Developmental Assessment and Intervention with Children and Adolescents

Ann Vernon, PhD

Department of Educational Administration
and Counseling
University of Northern Iowa
Cedar Falls, Iowa

AMERICAN
COUNSELING
ASSOCIATION

American Counseling Association
5999 Stevenson Avenue
Alexandria, VA 22304

Cover Design by Candy Levinson

Library of Congress Cataloging-in-Publication Data

Developmental assessment and intervention with children and adolescents /
  Ann Vernon.
    p. cm.
  Includes bibliographical references.
  ISBN 1-55620-122-2
  1. Children—Counseling of. 2. Youth—Counseling of.
3. Developmental psychology.
BF637.C6D48 1993
158'.3'083—dc20

                                                93-13261
                                                 CIP

Printed in the United States of America

TABLE OF CONTENTS

PREFACE

Over the past 25 years, we gradually have recognized that counseling children and adolescents is much different than counseling adults. With the realization that adult models of assessment and intervention cannot be extrapolated to young clients, numerous books, games, and articles have focused on what works with the child and adolescent population. More recently, a proliferation of information is available on how to help children of divorce; children of alcoholic parents; children who have been sexually, physically, or emotionally abused; or children who live in stepfamilies. Heavy emphasis also has been placed on how to work with suicidal, depressed, or chemically dependent youth.

In addition to these trends, helping professionals understand the importance of incorporating knowledge of child and adolescent development into the counseling process with a younger clientele. However, much of the emphasis on applying developmental theory to counseling children has been through comprehensive counseling programs that emphasize prevention through classroom and small-group work, rather than intervention and individual counseling.

This book, *Developmental Assessment and Intervention with Children and Adolescents*, was written to fill a void in the professional literature. Specifically, it addresses the individual counseling process with children and adolescents who exhibit more normal, developmental problems or typical problems in their age group, rather than serious problems such as suicide, depression, or addictive behaviors, which have been the focus of numerous recent publications. In addition, it summarizes information on developmental theory and combines it with a practical approach to both assessment and intervention with school-aged clients.

The first three chapters of this text discuss the special considerations and characteristics of developmental assessment and intervention with children and adolescents. Specific examples of assessment instruments and types of interventions are described. The remaining four chapters outline characteristics of normal development for four different age groups: early and middle childhood, and early and mid-adolescence. In each of these chapters, five case studies of typical problems are presented, followed by developmental assessment and intervention techniques that address the identified problem.

Developmental Assessment and Intervention with Children and Adolescents is intended for school and mental health counselors, social workers, and school psychologists who counsel children and adolescents and who want a practical resource to help them determine what the problem is, how it fits with the normal developmental sequence, and how to address the issue. It is also a book to help graduate students learn to combine theory and practice.

By reading this book, practitioners can learn how to help school-aged clients and significant others deal more effectively with the normal challenges of growing up. This publication is a welcome companion to those that apply developmental theory to prevention. It is my hope that *Developmental Assessment and Intervention with Children and Adolescents* can provide readers with practical information and user-friendly techniques to enhance their skills or give them new ideas in working with children and adolescents.

ACKNOWLEDGMENTS

I would like to thank the ACA Media Committee for inviting me to write this book, and, in particular, Dr. Loretta Bradley (Texas Tech University) and Dr. Richard Hayes (University of Georgia) for their helpful ideas. I also want to acknowledge Elaine Pirrone, former ACA acquisitions and development editor; Carolyn Baker, current ACA acquisitions and development editor; and Dr. Mark Hamilton, ACA director of communications and publications, for their assistance with this project. I also appreciated feedback from the reviewers, Dr. Richard Strub and Dr. Toni Tollerud, whose suggestions improved this manuscript.

Furthermore, I wish to thank my spouse, Nile, and son, Eric, as well as my family and close friends whose encouragement and support were invaluable throughout the writing of this book. Special appreciation goes to the counselor education faculty at the University of Northern Iowa, who assumed some of my responsibilities while I was on leave to write, and to my many young clients who continually affirm the importance of the helping profession as I see them grow through the counseling process.

ABOUT THE AUTHOR

Ann Vernon, Ph.D., N.C.C., is professor and coordinator of the counselor education program, Department of Educational Administration and Counseling, University of Northern Iowa, Cedar Falls, Iowa. Prior to her position as counselor educator, Dr. Vernon was an elementary and secondary counselor at the UNI Laboratory School. Dr. Vernon currently maintains a part-time private practice where she specializes in working with children, adolescents, and their parents.

In addition to teaching and counseling, Dr. Vernon is a frequent speaker at professional conferences and conducts workshops throughout the country on a variety of topics pertaining to children and adolescents. She is the author of *Thinking, Feeling, Behaving*, emotional education curriculums for children and adolescents, and has published numerous chapters in books on such topics as creative counseling techniques, group work, rational–emotive therapy with children, and self-development across the life span.

Dr. Vernon is the director of the Midwest Center for Rational–Emotive Therapy and a Fellow of the Institute for Rational–Emotive Therapy. She is current president-elect of North Central Association for Counselor Education and Supervision, and has been active in state, regional, and national counseling association activities.

INTRODUCTION

"I'm so concerned about my 6-year-old," explained a young parent to the school counselor. "She's been such a well-adjusted child, but suddenly she's convinced that there are monsters in her bedroom. She's terrified of the dark, and bedtime has become a catastrophe. I just don't understand why she's having these problems. As far as I can tell, everything else is fine at home and at school. I need to know what I can do to help her. Do you have any suggestions?"

"Our fourth grader's teacher suggested that we confer with you," expressed Jason's parents to the school counselor. "Jason isn't doing very well in school this year, and it's not because he doesn't have the ability. According to his teacher, Jason seems to think that he'll fail, no matter what. When he was younger he was very confident about his abilities, but during this past year, his performance has deteriorated and he just gives up before he really tries to figure things out. We don't know whether this is typical for this age, or whether we should have him evaluated? We know that we have to do something before the problem gets worse."

A frustrated father stated to a mental health counselor, "It's like we're living with a stranger! We've always been such a close family, but now our 14-year-old son doesn't even want to go on vacation with us because he'll miss spending time with his friends. And when he's not with them, he shuts himself off in his room. I remember doing some of that, and I know that kids change when they become teenagers, but is this normal?"

How does one know what is typical or normal? How does one determine the exact nature of the problem and what to do about it? The answers to these questions have significant implications for school counselors and other human development professionals, who routinely counsel children and adolescents and consult with parents and teachers to facilitate healthy development in a school-aged clientele. With increasing frequency, these professionals rely on developmental theories for direction in assessing and treating problems pertinent to childhood and adolescence. Drum and Lawler (1988) noted that, during the last 20 years, there has been heightened interest in developmental concepts, primarily due to three factors: (a) the increasing number of individuals who seek assistance for problems, many of which are developmentally related; (b) the realization that it is more cost-effective to help people deal with problems before they reach a crisis state; and (c) the concept of prevention, which emphasizes early education to prevent crisis. In addition, a developmental focus is the distinguishing characteristic of comprehensive school counseling programs (Gysbers & Henderson, 1988; Vernon & Strub, 1991). According to Borders and Drury (1992), "Effective counseling programs are clearly based in human development theories. . ." (p. 488). Interventions, curriculum, and student outcomes all should reflect developmental theories.

According to Ivey (1986), development is the goal of counseling. Drum and Lawler (1988) described it as "a gradual, life-long process of mental and emotional growth resulting from and necessary to the resolution of certain critical tasks, issues, or conflicts that characterize specific periods of the life span" (p. 5). Although development occurs by degrees, these authors contended that conscious attention and specific intervention are important to prevent or overcome problems that may block progression through the hierarchical stages of development. This intervention may be in the form of prevention, which is the primary focus of developmentally based school counseling programs (American School Counselor Association, 1984; Borders & Drury, 1992; Vernon & Strub, 1991). Although there is no major existing problem at the prevention level, programs are designed to educate students about the normal developmental process, help them anticipate probable conflicts and issues, and teach them coping strategies. The most common method of introducing prevention programs is through classroom guidance (Borders & Drury, 1992; Vernon & Strub, 1991).

Intervention also occurs at the individual or small-group level to help children overcome problems that are just beginning to emerge, or where there is an unmet need that is blocking the healthy developmental process. The focus at this level is on appropriate assessment to determine the specific issue, the severity and intensity of the problem, and effective interventions. Although education and prevention are also important, assessing the problem and selecting appropriate developmental interventions are the critical tasks.

In the case of recurring problems or more dysfunctional behavior, further assessment and directed intervention are imperative. Generally, problems of this nature are more serious than typical developmental problems, which can be ameliorated with less intense intervention.

The purpose of this book is to increase knowledge about child and adolescent development and the assessment of problems specific to this population. Intended as a guidebook for the practitioner, this material should help parents, teachers, human development professionals, and clients understand the nature of a problem from a developmental perspective; learn practical ways to assess the problem; and identify specific, developmentally appropriate interventions to assist with problem resolution. Following an overview of the assessment and intervention process, the chapters outline typical child and adolescent problems; developmental assessment procedures; and interventions for early childhood (ages 4–5), middle childhood (ages 6–11), early adolescence (ages 12–14), and mid-adolescence (ages 15–18). The primary focus is the application of developmental theory assessment and intervention in the individual counseling process.

REFERENCES

American School Counselor Association. (1984). *The school counselor and developmental guidance* (Position statement). Alexandria, VA: Author.

Borders, L., & Drury, S. (1992). Comprehensive school counseling programs: A review for policymakers and practitioners. *Journal of Counseling and Development, 70,* 487–498.

Drum, D., & Lawler, A. (1988). *Developmental interventions. Theories, principles, and practice.* Columbus, OH: Merrill.

Gysbers, N. C., & Henderson, P. (1988). *Developing and managing your school guidance program.* Alexandria, VA: American Association for Counseling and Development.

Ivey, A. E. (1986). *Developmental therapy.* San Francisco, CA: Jossey-Bass.

Vernon, A., & Strub D. (1991). *Developmental guidance program implementation.* Cedar Falls, IA: University of Northern Iowa Press.

PART I

CONCEPTS OF DEVELOPMENTAL THEORY, ASSESSMENT, AND INTERVENTION

There's a common saying that goes something like this: "If you don't know where you're going, you'll end up somewhere else." Although most counselors would agree that this makes sense, they do not automatically apply this wisdom within the context of the helping profession, particularly in terms of children and adolescents. In other words, although most professionals consider assessment and problem diagnosis as a prerequisite for determining intervention, this step is sometimes short-circuited with the child/adolescent population, because assessment may be defined too narrowly, it may be too time consuming, the instruments are not age-appropriate, the results do not readily translate to interventions, or the helping professional is unable to adequately engage the young client in the assessment process. As a result, this integral part of the counseling process may be overlooked, which, in turn, has a negative effect on the outcome.

The purpose of this book's first two chapters is to discuss the concept of developmental assessment as an effective assessment procedure with children and adolescents, and to underscore the importance of developmental theory in relation to assessment and intervention with young clients. More specifically, these chapters identify characteristics of effective child assessment, with particular emphasis on how to develop a variety of creative, practical assessment techniques to use with children and adolescents. Examples of existing developmental assessment instruments also are described.

In addition to the information on assessment, one chapter describes the intervention process, including a four-stage intervention design process, guidelines for selecting and creating developmentally appropriate interventions for younger clients, and specific types of interventions. A case study illustrates application of the design process.

As stated in the preface, I cannot merely extrapolate assessment procedures and intervention strategies to children and adolescents. The intent of the following chapters is to bridge the gap between theory and practice by providing practical ways to identify problems and concrete suggestions for what to do about them.

CHAPTER I

THE CHILD ASSESSMENT PROCESS

The importance of obtaining information directly from children and adolescents, rather than relying exclusively on behavioral observations or reports from parents, teachers, or other significant persons, has been recognized in recent years (Bierman, 1983; LaGreca, 1983; Stone & Lemanek, 1990). This recognition is due, in part, to an increased knowledge of the developmental process, which has resulted in a better understanding of the nature of childhood and the awareness that children are capable of providing data about their problems. Furthermore, there is growing acknowledgment that children are not simply miniature adults. As Yule (1981) cautioned, scaled-down versions of adult assessment techniques or adult models of normal/abnormal behavior cannot be applied to children. Because of children's uniquenesses, it is important to design appropriate assessment instruments that reflect the developmental capacities of children and to understand how the cognitive, emotional, and behavioral developmental processes impact the assessment process (Flanery, 1990).

Given the rapid changes that characterize early years, knowing what is developmentally appropriate is a prerequisite for identifying many childhood problems (LaGreca, 1990). For instance, 2-year-olds who express emotion by throwing temper tantrums are behaving rather normally, whereas 10-year-olds should be able to express emotions in more appropriate ways. Similarly, bed wetting may be a common problem for a 3-year-old, but not for a third grader. Understanding this age-appropriate behavior is critical in gaining perspective about problems characterizing childhood and adolescence.

THE NATURE OF ASSESSMENT

According to Hood and Johnson (1991), counseling is conceptualized as problem solving. It consists of a five-step model that includes problem

1

orientation, problem identification, generation of alternatives, decision making, and verification. These authors believe assessment provides information at each step of the model and is an integral part of the counseling process. Specifically, depending on the instrument, assessment increases sensitivity to problems, and, in fact, may be a way for individuals to deal with developmental issues before they become full-blown problems. In this way, assessment provides information for the client as well as for the professional conducting the assessment. Assessment procedures also are used to help clarify problems and determine the extent of the concern, as well as identify strengths that can be expanded on to enhance development.

The purpose of assessment with children is to identify needs and priorities that lead to recommendations that will enhance their lives and assist with the decision-making process (Goldman, Stein, & Guerry, 1983; Hood & Johnson, 1991). Assessment procedures can be a shortcut to learning about a child, but because different procedures produce different types of information, it is important to consider what type of information is needed before selecting a particular assessment instrument or procedure. In addition, it is essential to understand the importance of developmental processes and deviations from normal development, as well as how the child experiences the assessment process.

DEVELOPMENTAL ASSESSMENT

Developmental assessment emphasizes the assessment of individuals throughout the maturation process (Bradley, 1988). Instead of focusing solely on an individual at a particular age, developmental assessment is a broader concept that looks at specific characteristics within the context of the developmental sequence. As Bradley noted, "The approach is termed developmental assessment because it sees the aims of assessment, through various screening measures and instruments, as looking at how the individual moves through stages of development" (p. 136). The goal is to determine where the child or adolescent is in his or her development.

Developmental assessment focuses on the following characteristics (Drummond, 1992):

1. The normality of client functioning in areas such as: communication skills (verbal and nonverbal, listening and comprehension, receptive and expressive); cognitive skills (reasoning, thinking, memory, basic achievement, problem solving); physical development (gross and

fine motor skills, sensory development, general development); emotional development (temperament, adjustment, self-concept, attitudes, emotional expression); social development (interpersonal relationships with peers and family); self-care skills (ability to meet basic needs such as eating, drinking, dressing, toiletry); independent living skills (money management, functioning independently in home and community settings); work habits and adjustment (appropriate work habits and attitudes, job seeking and keeping abilities, ability to work independently and get along with others); and adjustment problems (aggression, hyperactivity, acting out, depression, stress, withdrawal).

2. The historical factors which positively or negatively impact functioning of the child.

3. How the current status of family and school issues contributes positively or negatively to overall functioning.

4. The physical, psychological, and emotional health of the client at present.

5. The educational, social, physical, and psychological needs.

6. The expectations of the client and significant others. From *Appraisal Procedures for Counselors and Helping Professionals* (2nd ed., pp. 206–207) by R.J. Drummond, 1992, New York: Macmillan Publishing Co. Copyright 1992 by Macmillan. Reprinted by permission.)

Another characteristic of developmental assessment is the emphasis on qualitative versus quantitative methods. Qualitative assessment usually is not a standardized test and there generally are not quantitative scores or tables that convert raw scores into percentile ranks or standard scores (Goldman, 1990). In a sense, qualitative methods are more "nontraditional," according to Goldman (1990, p. 205). Qualitative assessment emphasizes self-understanding within a developmental framework as well as a holistic approach, which avoids the specific measurement of the narrowly defined aspects of behavior, ability, or personality. Of particular importance is the fact that qualitative methods are not as precise as standardized tests, and the types of assessment procedures are more varied. Because of this, it is easier to adapt the method or the content to various ethnic, cultural, and sexual identity groups; to clients with disabilities; and to people from different socioeconomic levels.

A qualitative approach allows more active client involvement: "the client is not simply a 'passive responder' who is being measured, predicted, placed, or diagnosed" (Goldman, 1990, p. 205). This assures more client investment in the entire assessment and intervention process, which, in turn, results in more positive long-term effects. This type of assessment is also more dynamic rather than static, meaning that assessment is an ongoing process and that there is less distinction between assessment and intervention (Drummond, 1992). Thus, although some initial assumptions are made based on an assessment procedure administered early in the counseling process, this impression is tentative and may shift as new information is revealed in the course of counseling. Because developmental assessment is more ongoing, it diminishes some of the negative stigma about being "diagnosed and treated," and also is tied more closely to interventions. With this approach, the process of the counseling relationship does not have to be interrupted to give a standardized test.

In contrast to a structural, standardized assessment, which looks at how much or how little of a trait an individual possesses, the developmental approach looks for patterns and how these patterns relate to the total developmental process. In other words, rather than looking for a precise score, the developmental approach examines how the responses relate to the characteristics for a particular stage of development. For example, assessing self-esteem, the School Form of the Coopersmith Self-Esteem Inventory yields six scores (Hood & Johnson, 1991). Instead of using an instrument such as this to indicate how much or how little self-esteem a child has, the developmental approach might make use of a self-portrait to determine how the child's view of him or herself relates to stages of self-development.

Fadely and Hosler (1980) and Epanchin and Paul (1987) emphasized that developmental assessment should be comprehensive, including positive as well as deficit aspects of a child's functioning, so that the problem is assessed accurately from a total perspective. According to these authors, tests are given too often to determine what is wrong with a child, which results in a diagnosis of a disability, but may not provide an overall view of the nature of the child. "Merely giving tests is not enough. There has to be a more comprehensive means of establishing the competencies of the child" (Fadely & Hosler, 1980, p. 4). Drummond (1992) concurred with these authors, stressing that multiple measures of assessment allow the professional to combine information from a variety of sources. He suggested that, in addition to direct testing, naturalistic observation and interviews with significant others are also valuable assessment measures.

Differentiation of assessment levels is also important so that extensive, time-consuming assessment only is given when absolutely necessary, according to Fadely and Hosler (1980). In their opinion, assessment should not be complex, because this prevents problem resolution at a more basic level. They contended that it is more practical to use a "first-level" informal assessment procedure that does not authenticate a diagnosis, because so many assessment instruments do, but instead provides relevant information that can be used to structure an intervention program. This first-level assessment often includes teachers and/ or parents. Through involvement in the actual assessment, they tend to see the process as more valuable, and therefore invest more in the intervention process.

Developmental assessment is based on developmental psychology, which describes development as a process in which an individual gradually moves from the simple to the complex in interpersonal, emotional, moral, cognitive, and ego development (Berger & Thompson, 1991; Charlesworth, 1983; Elkind, 1980; Santrock & Yussen, 1992; Stone & Church, 1984). Although developmental theory generally has been characterized by an ordered sequence of stages, Drum and Lawler (1988) differentiated between those who describe the developmental process as involving internal change in the structure of the mind versus those who believe that it consists of a discrete number of phases. Those who adhere to the latter view refer to stages as tasks or challenges at particular periods during the life span. How these challenges are handled influences happiness and well-being, as well as success in negotiating future stages. For example, if a child does not learn to express feelings effectively, intimacy likely will become an issue in adulthood until this earlier task has been resolved successfully. Erik Erikson was one of the leading theorists of this point of view.

Piaget was the well-reknowned theorist who emphasized changes in the structure of the mind, whereas also ascribing to the concept of sequential stages. The changes that occur at each stage affect how one thinks, which in turn influence how an individual views the external world. Essentially, the focus is on how the mind changes in complexity and how this affects the integration and processing of information.

Although development usually is presented as a hierarchical concept, Ivey (1986) expanded this linear model by introducing the concept of recycling of stages, noting that development can be linear, cyclical, and spiraling. "We do develop in orderly progressions, we do seem to turn back on ourselves in repeating patterns, and yet the whole seems always more than the sum of its parts" (Ivey, 1986, p. 7). Thus, an individual may progress to a higher level, but simultaneously may rework issues from a previous stage, which leads to new understanding. Ivey's model incorporates the traditional stage sequence notion, and adds a new dimension that expands the theoretical concepts and seemingly reflects aspects of human growth and development more realistically.

Several developmental theorists' work has had a major impact on the nature of assessment across the life span. A brief overview is provided in the following section, with more in-depth coverage in subsequent chapters that specifically describes developmental stages and competencies corresponding to early and middle childhood and early and mid-adolescence.

DEVELOPMENTAL THEORIES

"Developmental theory is a systematic statement of principles that attempt to explain behavior and development" (Berger & Thompson, 1991, p. 33). Although this implies a universal pattern of development and that children who deviate from the norm are abnormal, Berger and Thompson noted that contemporary developmentalists rely on the principles as a general guideline, but also recognize uniquenesses, including gender and culture.

Cognitive Development

Jean Piaget was clearly a "giant" in the field of developmental psychology (Santrock & Yussen, 1992, p. 257). Piaget developed the conceptual framework that outlines key issues in cognitive development and emphasizes the development of rational thinking and stages of thought. Although environmental experiences are important, Piaget maintained that thoughts are the primary influence on children's actions (Berger & Thompson, 1991; Santrock & Yussen, 1992). He identified the following hierarchical stages of thought:

1. *Sensorimotor.* This stage corresponds with infancy, lasting from birth until about age 2. It is divided further into substages that describe changes in sensorimotor organization. Organizing and coordinating sensations with physical movements and developing object permanence occur in this stage.
2. *Preoperational thought.* During this period, ranging from approximately age 2 to age 7, mental reasoning emerges, stable concepts are formed, and egocentrism increases and then decreases. There are two substages: the symbolic function substage, in which the child is able to use symbols to represent objects; and the intuitive thought substage, in which the child begins to reason and is inquisitive.
3. *Concrete operational thought.* When children reach this stage at about age 7, they can reason logically and understand logical principles if they are applied to concrete examples (Berger & Thompson, 1991). Not only are they able to think more objectively, but they are able to understand concepts such as identity, reversibility, reciprocity, and classification. This stage ends at approximately age 11.

4. *Formal operations.* Between the ages of 11 and 15, formal operational thought, characterized by abstract thinking, develops. Formal operational thinkers are able to develop hypotheses and make conclusions about effective ways to solve problems. The two phases of formal operational thought, assimilation and accommodation, correspond with early and later stages of adolescence. Piaget concluded that formal operational thought is not achieved completely until later adolescence, ages 15–20 (Berndt, 1992; Santrock & Yussen, 1992; Sroufe & Cooper, 1988).

Ego-Development

Loevinger (1976) was credited with the majority of the work done on ego-development. She described a nine-stage model arranged in hierarchical order from the simple to the complex. Tasks at one stage must be accomplished before those at the next level can be initiated. The stages are as follows:

1. *Presocial stage.* The child sees no differentiation of self from environment.
2. *Impulsive stage.* Preoccupation with impulses (particularly sexual and aggressive) and a present orientation best describe this level of ego-development.
3. *Self-protective stage.* During this stage, the child blames circumstances or others for problems, and understands rules but uses them for personal gain. He or she learns to anticipate short-term reward and punishment.
4. *Conformist stage.* The child fears disapproval, perceives behavior as external, and is concerned about social acceptance, appearance, and reputation.
5. *Self-aware level.* At this level, there is an expanded consciousness of self and increasing appreciation of multiple possibilities in situations.
6. *Conscientious stage.* Characteristics of this stage include self-evaluation of goals, sense of responsibility and concern for others, and long-term perspectives.
7. *Individualistic stage.* A greater sense of individuality, need for emotional independence, and awareness of the conflict between personal needs and needs of others predominate this stage.
8. *Autonomous stage.* Individuals at this stage of development are able to recognize and handle conflict, allow others to be autonomous, and focus on self-fulfillment rather than on achievement.
9. *Integrated stage.* Although few people reach this stage, it could be described as an understanding of life's complexities.

Moral Development

"Moral development concerns rules and conventions about what people should do in their interactions with other people" (Santrock & Yussen, 1992, p. 585). How children think about rules, how they behave in moral circumstances, and how they feel about moral issues are critical factors.

Kohlberg (1980, 1984) and Gilligan (1982) have done extensive work on moral development. Kohlberg maintained that as children develop, their thoughts become more internally, rather than externally, controlled. Consistent with developmental theory, he believed that moral development consists of three levels, each characterized by two stages that are described as follows.

Level 1: Preconventional reasoning. The child has no internalization of moral values.

Stage 1: Punishment and obedience: children obey because they are told to; rewards and punishments govern moral reasoning.

Stage 2: Individualism and purpose: moral reasoning is based on rewards and self-interest; children obey when they want to or when they see it is in their best interests to do so.

Level 2: Conventional reasoning. Children obey others' standards and rules.

Stage 3: Interpersonal norms: children want to be seen as "good kids," adopting their parents' moral standards.

Stage 4: Social system morality: children make moral judgments based on their understanding of the law.

Level 3: Postconventional reasoning. At this stage, morality is not based on others' standards, but is internalized completely.

Stage 5: Community rights versus individual rights: the individual knows that laws are important, but thinks that some values are more important than laws.

Stage 6: Universal ethical principles: moral standards are based on universal human rights, so a person will follow his or her conscience even though there may be personal risk.

Another prominent moral development theorist, Gilligan (1982), argued that Kohlberg's model does not reflect a relationship perspective that females most often articulated. Gilligan developed the care perspective, which views people relative to their connectedness with others. The focus is on relationships with others, interpersonal communication, and care and concern for others. Gilligan based her theory on a three-stage model: preconventional morality (concern for self and survival), conventional morality (concern for caring for others and being responsible), and postconventional morality (concern for self and others are independent).

Both Colangelo (1982) and Yussen (1977) cautioned that, in assessing moral development in children, the content of the dilemmas and the types of problems must reflect everyday experiences and a diversity of problems.

Interpersonal Development

Selman (1980, 1981) is a prominent researcher in the development of interpersonal understanding. According to Cooney and Selman (1980), the development of interpersonal understanding is reflected in the concept of social perspective taking, which is a process that enables a person to take on the perspective of another and relate it to his or her own. Based on extensive investigation, Selman (1980) identified the following five-stage sequence of social perspective taking:

1. Stage 0: egocentric (up to age 6). The child can differentiate self and others, but not their points of view. There is no ability to relate perspectives. "People feel the way I would in that situation" would be characteristic of this stage (LeFrancois, 1992, p. 503).
2. Stage 1: social-informational (ages 6–8). Although the child realizes that people feel differently because they have different experiences or information, there is still the assumption that the correct perspective is his or her own.
3. Stage 2: self-reflective (ages 8–10). At this stage, the child is able to see that people can have different viewpoints and that no one perspective is absolutely right.
4. Stage 3: mutual (ages 10–12). The child in this stage talks about different points of view and can put him or herself in another's place to see it from that perspective.
5. Stage 4: social and conventional (ages 12–15+). The adolescent is able to use principles of the social system to analyze and evaluate his or her own perspective and those of others.

Psychosocial Development

Erikson (1963) formulated a comprehensive theory of development that emphasizes social and cultural influences. The interaction of social system support and individual characteristics are responsible for resolution of developmental conflicts. This theory provides a general framework for understanding changes that occur throughout development. There are eight stages in Erikson's model; the five that describe infancy, childhood, and adolescence are as follows.

1. Trust vs. mistrust (0–12 months). The primary task at this level is to develop trust that basic needs will be satisfied.
2. Autonomy versus shame and doubt (1–3 years). Developing a feeling of control over behavior and learning to be self-sufficient are critical tasks.
3. Initiative versus guilt (3–6 years). Children need to develop a sense of self, initiate activities, and assume a sense of responsibility for their actions.
4. Industry versus inferiority (7–11 years). Developing a sense of self-worth and competence through interaction with peers and their experiences is central to this stage.
5. Identity versus identity diffusion (adolescence). Establishing a strong sense of identity in a variety of dimensions is the principal developmental task at this level.

THE ASSESSMENT PROCESS WITH CHILDREN

Understanding how developmental levels impact the assessment process results in more effective assessment. More recently, the developmental literature has provided a better understanding of children, and, as a result, more emphasis has been placed on designing assessment procedures that are more appropriate for children and adolescents (Stone & Lemanek, 1990). Children are limited in their ability to comprehend or respond appropriately to some assessment instruments, and their lack of life experiences also restricts their understanding of various concepts. The following considerations are important:

1. Instruments must be constructed in language suitable to the child's reading and comprehension level.
2. Instruments and other assessment methods should reflect the attention span capability of the child.
3. The format of the assessment instrument or procedure should be appropriate. Stone and Lemanek (1990) reported that forced-choice formats are not very effective, because children are likely to select the last alternative. Likewise, a yes/no format usually is responded to with a "yes" by preschoolers.
4. To maintain a younger child's interest, pictures, cartoons, and other creative techniques need to be considered.
5. Questions that are relevant to the age, race, culture, or gender of the client facilitate attention to task and reflect sensitivity to persons from various groups.
6. The examples used in the assessment instrument must be appropriate to the life experiences of the child.

There are also some critical cognitive–developmental issues that have a major impact on the assessment process with children. Stone and Lemanek (1990) identified the following:

Emotional understanding . Regardless of the type of problem, assessing emotions generally is an important aspect of the evaluation procedure. Assessors often assume mistakenly that children can readily identify and express how they feel. However, the development of emotional understanding is progressive, and young children cannot report their emotions accurately (Stone & Lemanek, 1990). In soliciting information about feelings, the developmental level of emotional understanding is a crucial factor. The following information should serve as a helpful guideline.

The 4- to 6-year-olds can identify basic feelings accurately by observing facial expressions, although they sometimes confuse anger and sadness. Although they do not realize that feelings may be disguised or that they may be experienced simultaneously, children can communicate about simple emotions (Bretherton, Fritz, Zahn-Waxler, & Ridgeway, 1986).

As children get older, they understand that a person can have two conflicting emotions at the same time and rely more on their inner experiences or mental cues about what they or others are feeling. According to Carroll and Steward (1984), 8- and 9-year-olds understand that they can change their feelings as well as hide them. The 7- to 11-year-olds also recognize negative emotions. Although younger children see themselves as the major cause of their parents' emotions, by age 10 they realize that parents' emotions can be attributed to other people and events.

During adolescence, the understanding of emotions becomes more refined. Adolescents are able to understand the discrepancy between inner feelings and how these feelings are expressed. They are also able to make causal assumptions about feelings of others.

Concept of self. When children are asked to complete an assessment of some aspect of their functioning, it is assumed that they have enough of a sense of "self" that will make the assessment meaningful. This may not be the case, however, and it is important for the assessor to understand the development of self-concept.

Between the ages of 4 and 6, children tend to view the self as part of the body. There is an "all-or-none" conceptualization of personal traits and concrete descriptions of self based on behavior, activity, and physical appearance. From ages 7 to 11, children are able to incorporate psychological characteristics and social comparisons into self-descriptions, are aware of different components of self, and can differentiate between mental and physical aspects of self. The 12- to 16-year-olds are able to use abstract self-descriptions that are based on dispositions, values, and beliefs. Adolescents have a more integrated and consistent self-identity, and are capable of self-reflection and self-monitoring.

Because self-understanding progresses from the concrete and situation-specific to the abstract and psychological dimension of self, assessment instruments and procedures must employ more concrete, action-oriented questions for young children and then supplement this information with data from parents and teachers. At approximately 8 years of age, children have developed a more global sense of self and the assessment becomes more meaningful (Harter & Pike, 1984).

Person perception. The understanding of self and others appears to be interrelated (Damon & Killen, 1982). As with the development of the self-concept, there is a developmental progression relative to how others are perceived that needs to be considered when designing or using assessment instruments.

Stone and Lemanek (1990) depicted 4- to 6-year-olds as capable of describing another person's behavior, but not of explaining the behavior. At this age, descriptions of others tend to be very concrete, such as "Eric has a puppy" or "Shelley called me a name." There is confusion in the children's understanding of what actions are intentional versus accidental (Schantz, 1983).

Next, 7- to 11-year-olds can describe others relative to personal and psychological characteristics, but they still are not aware that others can have both positive and negative qualities. They are able to see that factors such as ability might be related to outcome, and they compare their feelings and thoughts to those of others (Selman, 1980).

Adolescents are able to make psychological comparisons; relate interests, abilities, and beliefs; and can explain and predict another person's behavior based on a mutual perspective and societal concepts (Selman, 1980). The adolescents' description of others is more complex.

This gradual shift from the concrete to the abstract in describing how others are perceived has implications for the assessment process. If asked to describe relationships with others, the preschooler will give a concrete response about physical appearance or a behavior, whereas the adolescent will explain dispositional causes of behavior and more complex relationship factors (Stone & Lemanek, 1990).

Language skills. The quality of information obtained from a child obviously is influenced by the ability to communicate. Like other areas of development, language acquisition proceeds in a sequential order.

By age 5, the basic dimensions are well developed (Bee, 1992). However, it is important to remember that children have more limited comprehension, which affects the assessment process. Likewise, their experiences are not as expansive and they may not have the necessary vocabulary to describe situations. The assessment instrument must reflect the appropriate reading level.

CHARACTERISTICS OF EFFECTIVE CHILD ASSESSMENT

Awareness of Developmental Issues

Developmental issues have a definite impact on the assessment process with school-aged children in several significant ways. First, without an understanding of what is normal at various stages of development, problems can be misconstrued and taken out of context. The following case illustrates this issue.

Andrew, a high school junior, was referred to a counselor by his parents, who were extremely concerned about his relationship with a young woman. His mother stated, "Andrew is much too preoccupied with this relationship. He limits his hours at work so that he can spend time with her. He never sees his buddies, and he has lost interest in his usual activities." What blew the problem "out of the water" was when Andrew left several notes lying around in his room and his mother happened to glance at one as she put clothes away. She panicked at the references to sexual desires and immediately limited the amount of time he could spend with his girlfriend. This, in turn, angered Andrew, and a series of intense family arguments ensued. The parents, convinced that he was sexually active on a regular basis, met with the girlfriend's parents, urging them to also restrict the involvement. Jane's parents maintained that this was a normal teenage relationship and had no intention of complying with their request.

When the parents called to set up an appointment for Andrew, the counselor suggested that the three of them attend the session. After meeting first with Andrew, it seemed as if his parents had blown the problem out of proportion. Yes, he professed to love Jane, wanted to be with her constantly, and was struggling with his desire to be sexual with her. After an open discussion and sharing of one of the notes with the counselor, it was apparent that Andrew was wrestling with normal developmental issues, as were his parents. "Letting go" is a critical task for parents at this stage in an adolescent's development, and exploring a sexual identity and developing an intimate relationship are primary tasks for the teenager. Had the parents been more aware of adolescent development, there might not have been the overreaction. Certainly concern about the relationship was appropriate, but jumping to conclusions based on sexual innuendos in a note definitely distorted the issue.

As this case illustrates, awareness of developmental tasks and stages helps put a problem in perspective, and perhaps circumvents extensive assessment and intensive intervention. Several other characteristics of effective child assessment are described subsequently.

Problem Identification

In problem assessment, it is important to distinguish between practical and emotional problems (Bernard & Joyce, 1984; Grieger & Boyd, 1980). Practical problems relate to external or environmental events and typically involve difficulty in managing, adapting to, or solving specific problems in the environment. Examples of practical problems for children or adolescents might include poor study habits, aggressive rather than assertive behavior with a friend, not knowing how to be self-sufficient if left at home alone, or not knowing where to find information about a specific career. Practical problems involve behavioral skill deficits, lack of information, inadequate problem-solving skills, or unrealistic environmental demands.

Emotional problems are undesirable emotions about the practical problem and interfere with the client's ability to solve the practical problem. Examples of emotional problems include feeling guilty about poor grades resulting from bad study habits, feeling angry about mishandling a relationship problem, or feeling ashamed for not readily knowing what to do or where to access information. Emotional reactions add another layer to the problem and must be assessed and addressed for the problem to be resolved.

It is also critical to assess the frequency, intensity, and duration of the symptoms. The Frequency Intensity Duration (FID) Scale (Bernard & Joyce, 1984) is a useful technique for determining the severity of the problem. By identifying the frequency with which the problem occurs, the intensity and duration of the response, and how long the problem has been evident, the practitioner develops a realistic perception of the problem, which in turn is useful in determining the level of further assessment and intervention. This is also helpful for parents, because, as is frequently the case, parents who refer a child for counseling are somewhat anxious and may unintentionally exaggerate the extent of the concern. For example, I recently consulted with an 8-year-old's parents who were convinced that the child was not working up to his potential and would get bad grades throughout school. In probing further, this above-average ability child recently had gotten a failing grade on one test, and that was the extent of it. By looking at the frequency of the bad marks, which in this case was one, and comparing it to his other grades and to his potential, it was determined that the problem was not occurring frequently enough to warrant further assessment or intervention. It would have been different had this become a pattern where the grades had been declining over a period of time in more than one class. Using the FID Scale is invaluable in obtaining a clear picture of the issue.

Involvement of Significant Others in the Assessment Process

Promoting a problem-solving approach and mutual participation to address concerns of parents, professionals, and children is an extremely important criteria of effective assessment. LaGreca (1990) listed several reasons: (a) the child's behavior may be situation-specific, and it is important to evaluate it within the broader social context; (b) the child generally is referred by parents or teachers, and therefore it is critical to obtain their perspective in addition to the child's; and (c) these significant persons such as parents and teachers typically are involved in some phase of the intervention process. Fadely and Hosler (1980) contended that including parents and teachers in some phase of the assessment process helps them better understand the child.

Not only does one develop a better understanding of the child from the adults in his or her life, but one also obtains a more accurate understanding of the problem. In many cases, although the child manifests the symptom, the problem lies within the environment. For example, consider the child who is referred by the classroom teacher for disruptive behavior. It may be true that the child is disruptive, but unless some assessment is made of the system, the practitioner may try to "fix" the child, never realizing that this child is not the only one who is disruptive in an ineffectively managed classroom.

Involving significant others is important for the reasons stated earlier, but it is also often essential to the assessment process to get an accurate representation of the problem, as the following case demonstrates.

Fifteen-year-old Nina was having problems dealing with her anger. There were frequent, explosive parent–child conflicts that usually occurred when Nina's parents denied her requests to stay out later, do something with friends, spend money, or asked her to assume some responsibilities at home. As an only child, Nina had been used to getting her way, but as she got older and was requesting more freedom, her parents were setting curfews and placing reasonable limits on what she could or could not do. They also had decided that they were no longer going to give in to Nina's demands, and this usually resulted in a temper tantrum.

Initially during counseling sessions, Nina was very open about the conflicts and willingly worked on her anger. Several family sessions were held and things improved. However, knowing that change does not occur overnight, the counselor continued to meet with Nina to develop anger management techniques further. After a session or two, Nina kept insisting that everything was fine and that she had not had problems at all with anger. Therefore, it was rather surprising when the counselor received an urgent phone call from Nina's mother indicating lots of recent conflict and that Nina's anger often was very out of control.

The moral to the story? Children and adolescents may, for a variety of reasons, distort the extent of the problem. This may have to do with shame (what does it say about me if I have problems?), confusion and anxiety (am I "sick" because I'm in counseling?), hopelessness (this won't help anyway), or ownership (it's not my problem, it's their's). It also may reflect the child's inability to specifically express how the problem affects him or her. Whatever the cause, involving others in various aspects of the assessment process results in more accurate problem assessment (Epanchin & Paul, 1987).

The Assessment Relationship

Because children and adolescents often do not "own" the problem, do not refer themselves for counseling, or do not understand the purpose and process of the assessment, they may resist or be reluctant. This may be manifested in a continuum of behavior from overt unwillingness or refusal to cooperate to acceptance and compliance. Even if the child is in counseling willingly, it is essential to establish a sound working relationship and to employ strategies that are more effective for a younger clientele. The following suggestions may be helpful.

The preschool child. After introducing yourself to the child and indicating that you are glad he or she is here, it often is effective to share a toy or play a game with a child of this age, particularly if you sense discomfort: "Joshua, if you'd like to, you can hold this cuddly stuffed elephant." Providing a simple explanation of the reason for the visit and "normalizing" the problem also is important to alleviate anxiety: "Joshua, your mom wanted you to come to see me because she knows that it's hard for you to go outside or up to your bedroom because you're afraid of being alone. I've worked with several kids who feel like this." Some informal discussion about family members, pets, or friends also can facilitate rapport building. If the child is extremely shy or reluctant, it may be good to invite the parent(s) into the interview room. Verbal praise or a reward such as a sticker is appropriate at this age for re-inforcing cooperative behavior and attention to task.

The elementary school child. Following an introduction of yourself and a basic description of what you do, it is important to ask the child if he or she knows why he or she is meeting with you, how he or she feels about it, and if he or she has any questions. If the child seems unclear about the purpose of the visit, it is best to be straightforward: "Your dad told me that you were having some problems adjusting to your new baby sister. He brought you here so that I could learn more about the problem and we could figure out some ways to help you. What do you think about that?" It is also a good idea to advise parents about what to say to the child about visiting with you. For instance, if your title is "Dr." the child may think that you are a medical doctor and that he or she is going to you for a shot, as one 8-year-old client recently shared. If both the professional and the parent can clarify misconceptions, it is easier to establish the relationship.

Playing a board game such as checkers or Sorry (Parker Brothers) often is effective. This author prefers to use more personalized games or strategies that yield more personal data about the child. Six- to 9-year-olds like "Who Are You?" (Vernon, self-developed):

> *Dr. V.:* "Let's play a short game to help us get better acquainted. You can ask me 'Who Are You?' and I'll give you an answer. Then I'll ask you, and you can ask me, and we'll continue for awhile until we learn some things about each other."
> *Danielle:* "Who are you?"
> *Dr. V.:* "I'm a dog lover. I have three Golden Retrievers. Who are you?"
> *Danielle:* "I like pets too. I have a rabbit and two fish. Who are you?"

The information obtained from this simple game can be used in subsequent sessions to reestablish the relationship. "Tell me something funny that your rabbit did this week" sets the client at ease and shows her that she's important because you remember things about her.

The adolescent. An adolescent often is reluctant to attend counseling and participate in problem assessment. Do not expect the adolescent to "own" the problem, to be eager to deal with it, or to like you. With adolescents, it is best to be direct and honest about who you are, what you do, and to listen to their feelings about being with you. "Your mom told me that you didn't want to come today. I understand that, but I would like to try and help you work on the problem with your depression. I have several other clients your age, and by working together, they began to feel better. Some of them felt like they were "sick" or "crazy" because they were here.... Do you feel that way?" Although an adolescent may not raise this concern about being different or sick, it generally is a fear, and bringing it out in the open is reassuring. Acknowledging an adolescent's resistance and indicating that he or she does not have to like coming, but perhaps can tolerate it for at least a few times, is a strategy that seems to work well with this age group. Demystifying the assessment process by avoiding the use of the word *test* is recommended.

Shy or hostile client. It may be too intimidating to begin an interview with a shy client by immediately attempting to assess the problem. A more informal, conversational approach might be best: learning more about the client's interests, pastimes, favorite teams, or musical groups (Oster, Caro, Eagen, & Lillo, 1988). Playing a game can help a shy client feel more at ease. With this type of client, it is important not to "push" the process. Often the more intense the approach, the more the shy child backs away. Patience pays off in the end.

A hostile client, most often an adolescent, presents a professional challenge. Characteristically he or she denies problems, is unwilling to reveal personal information, and is guarded and suspicious. Remember that fear and anxiety usually underlie the anger and the hostile behavior that protects him or her from being too vulnerable. With this client, it is best to proceed slowly, listen to his or her perspective, and take it seriously. Despite that there may be distortions in his or her thinking, a hostile client often can be engaged by helping him or her see that you can intervene in the family system, if that is creating part of the problem, and that you can give specific techniques for dealing with anger, because that is creating further problems. The following case is an example of this approach.

Twelve-year-old Kevin was extremely hostile and had only come for his appointment after his parents had given him the choice of meeting with me or going to the hospital. Knowing that he was very resistant, I told him that I wanted to hear his "side" of the story so that we could determine what was causing his problems. Immediately he volunteered that he should not be seeing me because his parents had the problem. I acknowledged that could very well be true and that I also would be working with them. This seemed to reduce the hostility somewhat. I then indicated that I needed to get some idea of the frequency and intensity of his anger and how he behaved when he was angry. He once again insisted that if his parents knew how to be better parents, he wouldn't have to get angry. "Kevin, I'm sure you're right, but so far you haven't been able to change their behavior by getting angry. In fact, I'll bet it just gets you in more trouble, right?" He nodded his head, but insisted that he had no other choice. I told him that I understood that, but knew from past experience in working with other kids who had similar problems that there were some things he could do to better express the anger so that he wouldn't have to be punished by his parents all the time. Then, once he'd accomplished that, he could work on ways to change them. This strategy did deescalate the hostility, and during the second session we were able to get into the problem assessment process.

Some additional rapport builders with all clients:

1. Explain to the child how the information obtained from the assessment process can be used to facilitate problem solving.
2. Use humor where appropriate to help establish a more comfortable relationship.
3. Find out about hobbies, favorite teams, school activities, and favorite pastimes. Use this knowledge to "chit chat" in the first few minutes of the session.
4. For a young child, have smaller furniture if possible. Create an inviting, but not overly stimulating or cluttered, environment.
5. Be yourself. It is important to be personal, but not an overly friendly "buddy" (Oster et al., 1988).
6. Flexibility, empathy, openness, and patience are essential in establishing a relationship with a child.
7. Show genuine interest and concern for the client.
8. Take leads from the client. If you sense that he or she is more comfortable on the floor, don't restrict yourself to your chair. By all means, don't sit behind a desk even when conferring with parents, because this creates distance and inhibits a collaborative relationship.

Cultural Sensitivity

Given that we live in a multicultural society, it is imperative that we consider how culture affects the assessment process. Certainly the practitioner views the situation or information through his or her own cultural perspective. For example, most North Americans would consider it rude if a parent came to a conference 30 minutes late, and might infer negative things about the parent's commitment. To many Latin Americans, this would be normal behavior with no negative implications.

Communication style also is culturally related. In an interview situation, a child might not respond to questions, because, in his or her culture, certain things are not discussed with relative strangers. McAdoo (1977) noted that Black families are particularly reluctant to discuss family problems outside the family. Eye contact is another example. Although valued by White middle-class Americans, the Native American culture sees this as a sign of disrespect (Wise & Miller, 1989).

"The culturally sensitive professional looks for the parallels in the behaviors of children of various groups, while still appreciating the differences between the groups' perceptions of the world" (Garbarino & Stott, 1989, p. 94). These authors noted that although all people share similar problems, different cultures define situations and circumstances differently. For example, they cited an inner-city adolescent who lies to cover for a powerful gang member, contrasted with a suburban child who lives in a safe environment but lies to a friend. Although both lie, one does it in response to a threat for survival and the other to avoid a friend's disapproval.

Gender roles, ethnicity, and social class are other important variables to consider in the assessment process. Each culture defines its gender roles, and what is considered normal in one culture may vary significantly in another. The strong maternal role characteristic of Black families and the macho Hispanic male are not found, for the most part, in mainstream White communities (McAdoo, 1981). The practitioner must be careful not to make judgments based on his or her own cultural orientation. Ethnicity and social class differences need to be considered when selecting assessment instruments so the child can relate to what is being asked.

Several other dimensions impact the assessment process as well. Cultural groups have different definitions of such factors as: (a) discipline and caregiving: what one culture perceives as abusive, another may see as good firm discipline (Gray & Cosgrove, 1985); (b) health and illness: different groups vary in their ideas about the causes of illnesses and how to treat them; and (c) personal-institutional relationships: maintaining close family relationships is more important than the system (Garbarino & Stott, 1989). Understanding how different groups experience such factors has direct bearing on the outcome of assessment.

ETHICAL CONSIDERATIONS

Regardless of what is being assessed and how, practitioners must respect the feelings of young clients and acknowledge that they may be resistant or reluctant because they do not understand the process. Although developmental assessment often tends to be more informal and is tied to the intervention process, children still may be anxious about participating, particularly if the referral comes from the parent or teacher. It is the helping professional's ethical responsibility to establish a good working relationship with the client and to conduct the assessment in a respectful manner.

Although it is not the intent of this chapter to present a detailed coverage of ethics, some specific issues arise when working with younger clients. For instance, the assessment process may have a negative emotional impact on children. If children respond to questions about their worries, fears, or peer relations, will they become more distressed? Although Burbach, Farha, and Thorpe (1986) noted that little empirical data exist to support this concern, practitioners should approach the assessment process in a sensitive manner, carefully explaining the purpose and procedures to the children.

Second is the issue of confidentiality. Ordinarily assessment data are considered professional information and are not disclosed to others without client consent (Hood & Johnson, 1991). However, with younger clients, it is generally essential to share results at least with parents. Children need to be informed prior to the assessment that the practitioner probably will communicate to some extent with parents and/or teachers, because they most likely will be involved in helping the children resolve the problems. Emphasizing to the children that the purpose of the assessment is to gain information to help them deal more effectively with the concern often circumvents this issue. Furthermore, because the developmental assessment process often is not as structured or explicit as other assessments, children may be more receptive to having information shared because there is not a score that categorizes them.

As in any counseling situation, professionals have an obligation to only use those instruments or techniques that they are qualified to administer. Furthermore, they need to use methods that are appropriate for children and consider how the results will be used.

SUMMARY

As the importance of developmental factors becomes more widely acknowledged, professionals will rely more on developmental assessment with children and adolescents for the following reasons.

1. It provides more useful, relevant information. Instead of a test score, which may only confirm a loosely formulated diagnosis, these assessment data can be tied more readily to interventions and problem resolution.
2. It is more culture and gender sensitive, because the instruments and assessment methods are modified more easily.

3. It looks at the problem within the total context of development and helps define what is *normal.*
4. It can be less threatening to younger clients, because a variety of assessment techniques may be used to determine the specific nature of the problem.
5. It involves significant others in the assessment process, which in turn assures their more active participation in the intervention phases.
6. It encompasses a wide variety of assessment procedures that can be adapted more readily to match the age of the client.

REFERENCES

Bee, H. (1992). *The developing child.* New York: HarperCollins.

Berger, K., & Thompson, R. (1991). *The developing person through childhood and adolescence.* New York: Worth.

Bernard, M., & Joyce, M. (1984). *Rational–emotive therapy with children and adolescents.* New York: Wiley.

Berndt, T. (1992). *Child development.* Orlando, FL: Harcourt Brace Jovanovich.

Bierman, K. (1983). Cognitive development and clinical interviews with children. In B. B. Lahey & A. E. Kazdin (Eds.), *Advances in clinical child psychology* (Vol. 6, pp. 217–250). New York: Plenum.

Bradley, L. (1988). Developmental assessment: A life-span process. In R. Hayes & R. Aubrey (Eds.), *New directions for counseling and human development* (pp. 137–157). Denver, CO: Love Publishing.

Bretherton, I., Fritz, J., Zahn-Waxler, C., & Ridgeway, D. (1986). Learning to talk about emotions: A functionalist perspective. *Child Development, 57,* 529–548.

Burbach, D. J., Farha, J. G., & Thorpe, J. S. (1986). Assessing depression in community samples of children using self-report inventories: Ethical considerations. *Journal of Abnormal Child Psychology, 14,* 579–589.

Carroll, J., & Steward, M. (1984). The role of cognitive development in children's understanding of their own feelings. *Child Development, 55,* 1486–1492.

Charlesworth, R. (1983). *Understanding child development.* Albany, NY: Delmar.

Colangelo, N. (1982). Characteristics of moral problems as formulated by gifted adolescents. *Journal of Moral Education, 11,* 219–232.

Cooney, E. W., & Selman, R. (1980). Children's use of social conceptions: Toward a dynamic model of social cognition. *Personnel and Guidance Journal, 58,* 345–352.

Damon, W., & Killen, M. (1982). Peer interaction and the process of change in children's moral reasoning. *Merrill-Palmer Quarterly, 28,* 347–367.

Drum, D., & Lawler, A. (1988). *Developmental interventions: Theories, principles, and practice.* Columbus, OH: Merrill.

Drummond, R. (1992). *Appraisal procedures for counselors and helping professionals.* New York: Merrill.

Elkind, D. (1980). Child development and counseling. *Personnel and Guidance Journal, 58*, 353–355.

Epanchin, B., & Paul, J. (1987). *Emotional problems of childhood and adolescence: A multidisciplinary perspective.* Columbus, OH: Merrill.

Erikson, E. H. (1963). *Childhood and society* (2nd ed.). New York: Norton.

Fadely, J., & Hosler, V. (1980). *Developmental psychometrics: A resource book for mental health workers and educators.* Springfield, IL: Charles C. Thomas.

Flanery, R. (1990). Methodological and psychometric considerations in child reports. In A. LaGreca (Ed.), *Through the eyes of the child: Obtaining self-reports from children and adolescents* (pp. 57–82). Boston: Allyn & Bacon.

Garbarino, J., & Stott, F. (1989). *What children can tell us.* San Francisco, CA: Jossey-Bass.

Gilligan, C. (1982). *In a different voice.* Cambridge, MA: Harvard University Press.

Goldman, J., Stein, C., & Guerry, S. (1983). *Psychological methods of child assessment.* New York: Brunner/Mazel.

Goldman, L. (1990). Qualitative assessment. *The Counseling Psychologist, 18*, 205–213.

Gray, E., & Cosgrove, D. (1985). Ethnogentric perception of childrearing practices in protective services. *Child Abuse and Neglect, 9*, 389–396.

Greiger, R., & Boyd, J. (1980). *Rational-emotive therapy: A skills-based approach.* New York: Van Nostrand Reinhold.

Harter, S., & Pike, R. (1984). The pictorial scale of perceived competence and social acceptance for young children. *Child Development, 55*, 1969–1982.

Hood, A., & Johnson, R. (1991). *Assessment in counseling: A guide to the use of psychological assessment procedures.* Alexandria, VA: American Association for Counseling and Development.

Ivey, A. (1986). *Developmental therapy.* San Francisco, CA: Jossey-Bass.

Kohlberg, L. (1980). *The meaning and measurement of moral development.* Worcester, MA: Clark University Press.

Kohlberg, L. (1984). *The psychology of moral development.* San Francisco, CA: Harper & Row.

LaGreca, A. (1983). Interviewing and behavioral observations. In C. E. Walker & M. C. Roberts (Eds.), *Handbook of clinical child psychology* (pp. 109–193). New York: Wiley.

LaGreca, A. (1990). *Through the eyes of the child: Obtaining self-reports from children and adolescents.* Boston: Allyn & Bacon.

LeFrancois, G. R. (1992). *Of children: An introduction to child development.* Belmont, CA: Wadsworth.

Loevinger, J. (1976). *Ego development.* San Francisco, CA: Jossey-Bass.

McAdoo, H. (1977). Family therapy in the black community. *Journal of the American Orthopsychiatric Association, 47*, 75–79.

McAdoo, H. (1981). *Black families.* Newbury Park, CA: Sage.

Oster, G., Caro, J., Eagen, D. R., & Lillo, M. (1988). *Assessing adolescents.* New York: Pergamon.

Santrock, J., & Yussen, S. R. (1992). *Child development: An introduction.* Dubuque, IA: William C. Brown.

Schantz, C. U. (1983). Social cognition. In P. Mussen (Ed.), *Handbook of child psychology* (Vol. 3, pp. 455–495). New York: Wiley.

Selman, R. (1980). *The growth of interpersonal understanding: Developmental and clinical analyses.* New York: Academic Press.

Selman, R. (1981). The child as a friendship philosopher. In S. R. Asher & J. M. Gottman (Eds.), *The development of children's friendships* (pp. 242–272). New York: Cambridge University Press.

Sroufe, L. A., & Cooper, R. G. (1988). *Child development: Its nature and course.* New York: Knopf.

Stone, J., & Church, J. (1984). *Childhood and adolescence.* New York: Random House.

Stone, W., & Lemanek, K. (1990). Developmental issues in children's self-reports. In A. LaGreca (Ed.), *Through the eyes of the child: Obtaining self-reports from children and adolescents* (pp. 18–56). Boston: Allyn & Bacon.

Wise, F., & Miller, N. (1989). The mental health of the American Indian child. In J. Garbarino & F. Stott (Eds.), *What children can tell us* (pp. 92–107). San Francisco, CA: Jossey-Bass.

Yule, W. (1981). The epidemiology of child psychopathology. In B. B. Lahey & A. E. Kazdin (Eds.), *Advances in clinical child psychology* (Vol. 4, pp. 1–51). New York: Plenum.

Yussen, S. R. (1977). Characteristics of moral dilemmas written by adolescents. *Developmental Psychology, 13,* 162–163.

CHAPTER II

METHODS OF
DEVELOPMENTAL ASSESSMENT

By definition, developmental assessment is qualitative in nature. With this approach, one does not simply give a test and report the results. Rather, there is an interactive element between assessment and the counseling process. A distinguishing characteristic of developmental assessment is its reliance on developmental theory, which describes how individuals change and grow (Bradley, 1988).

Developmental assessment is particularly appropriate with children and adolescents, because, during this period of life, tremendous developmental changes occur. Tying the assessment process to the developmental framework provides a more accurate sense of (a) how the child is moving through stages of development, and (b) where and to what extent intervention should occur.

The purpose of this chapter is to describe the development of appropriate assessment procedures that can be used with children and adolescents, to identify existing developmental instruments, and to present a model that incorporates a developmentally based approach.

DESIGNING DEVELOPMENTAL ASSESSMENT INSTRUMENTS

Although commercial developmental assessment instruments exist and can be used as formal evaluation or screening devices, many of these instruments are designed more specifically for infants or very young children and assess a broad spectrum of abilities to determine readiness or placement (Bradley, 1988; Drummond, 1992; Guidubaldi, DeZolt, & Myers, 1991). These instruments emphasize performance in speech and language development, fine and gross motor development, perceptual development, physical development, and cognitive and self-help skills. However, parents, teachers, and children often want to know where children "fit" relative to more typical developmental problems, such as the things they worry about, the amount of independent behavior they exhibit, or their level of self-esteem. Although instruments measuring social–emotional development exist, many are designed specifically for very young children or do not address appropriately some of the more common questions that parents, teachers, or children have about development. For this reason, practitioners need to know how to design more informal assessment procedures that may be less structured, but nevertheless provide relevant data about other issues related to growth and development.

These more informal assessment procedures may yield results that can be used for effective intervention, or they might need to be paired with a commercially developed instrument for a more comprehensive picture of the problem.

Practitioner-designed procedures may assume a variety of formats, which allows a better "fit" with the client's learning style, verbal ability, emotional maturity, gender, or cultural background. Examples of assessment tools that can be developed include:

1. Checklists or rating scales of developmental characteristics.
2. Unfinished sentences.
3. Writing activities.
4. Decision-making dilemmas.
5. Games.
6. Art activities.
7. Story-telling and bibliotherapy techniques.
8. Self-monitoring techniques.
9. Role-play activities.
10. Play therapy strategies.

Checklists or Rating Scales of Developmental Characteristics

Depending on the client's age, a checklist or rating scale might be given to parents or teachers, to the client, or to the client and the adult(s). Checklists can be constructed simply by listing characteristics that relate to the initial identified concern. For instance, if parents are questioning whether their 10-year-old is developing appropriate social skills, the practitioner could refer to stages of interpersonal development (Selman, 1980, 1981), describe social skills characteristic of children at this age, and give the parents a checklist. The checklist might include questions such as:

> Does your child seem to be aware of others' feelings? (Example: My teacher was really mad.)
> Is your child able to see social situations from more than just his or her point of view? (Example: I didn't get invited to the party, but maybe his parents would only let him invite a few kids.)

Does your child understand that if he or she helps a friend, a friend might in turn help him or her? (Example: If I lend you a book, maybe you'll let me borrow your new tape.)

Is your child able to recognize and avoid statements that might be potentially offensive to others? (Example: She wears ugly clothes.)

Is your child able to recognize personality characteristics in others? (Example: He is shy; she is bossy.)

This checklist also could be modified to include a rating scale. Rather than responding with a yes or no, a 1–5 scale could represent low to high dimensions of a particular characteristic.

Unfinished Sentences

Unfinished sentences elicit responses that help identify concerns and stages of development. If you are attempting to assess a 10-year-old's level of self-worth, sentences based on five areas, in which children evaluate their self-worth (Harter, 1988), could provide useful information:

1. When I don't do well on a test, I feel _____.
2. If my friend runs faster or plays sports better than I do, it means that _____.
3. If I misbehave in class, I feel _____.
4. If I don't get invited to a party, I think _____.
5. When I look in a mirror, I _____.

By designing questions that address the five areas of self-worth (scholastic competence, athletic competence, behavioral conduct, social acceptance, and physical appearance), the practitioner can develop a sense of how the child sees him or herself. By comparing the responses to what developmental theorists have determined is characteristic of children at this particular age, you have a picture of what is normal as well as areas that need strengthening.

Depending on the child's age, the youngster may complete the sentences on paper independently or the questions could be read to the child and the responses recorded.

Writing Activities

Through various writing activities, it is possible to identify patterns that can be compared to developmental stages. Diaries; logs; journals; and self-composed songs, poems, and stories are excellent sources of information that assist in the assessment and intervention processes. Depending on the type of writing activity, this form of assessment may be more appropriate for academically gifted students and adolescents. Examples of writing assignments that can be used to assess a variety of factors include:

1. Journal entries illustrating feelings and triggering events that occurred throughout the week.
2. A written analysis of songs that they think describe how they see themselves.
3. Self-composed short stories or poems that identify moral dilemmas or decision-making issues.
4. Self-composed songs that describe personal or social relationship concerns.

Decision-Making Dilemmas

How children and adolescents make decisions is influenced by stages of moral development. By designing dilemmas that require the young client to make a decision, it is possible to assess the decision-making process, understand why certain decisions are made based on stages of moral reasoning (Kohlberg, 1981), and design intervention strategies to facilitate more effective decision-making skills. In developing effective dilemmas, consider characteristic issues for the targeted client. Yussen (1977) identified interpersonal relationships, physical safety, and stealing as key moral dilemma topics for young adolescents. Based on this information, the following describes a decision-making dilemma for an adolescent client.

You and two friends are in a clothing store looking at sweatshirts. Before going to the mall, one of your friends indicated that she didn't have any money. At school the next day, you notice this friend is wearing one of the sweatshirts that she looked at yesterday in the store. You're sure her parents didn't buy it for her, because she stayed at your house until after the stores closed because her folks were out of town.

After reading the dilemma, engage the client in a series of questions: Assuming that this friend stole the sweatshirt, what do you think about what she did? Should you do anything about it? If so, what are your options?

Based on the responses, it is possible to determine the approximate stage of moral development. For instance, most adolescents are in what Kohlberg characterized as the conventional stage of moral development (Santrock & Yussen, 1992). As such, they believe that stealing is wrong because there are laws against it, but they also use loyalty to others as a basis of moral judgment. Therefore, they may not consider turning in their friend to authorities or telling the parents, because this is not in keeping with what a good friend would do. Once this developmental level has been assessed, interventions can be identified to help clarify the issue and look at alternative ways to deal with the problem.

Games

For younger children, in particular, various types of simple games can be used in the problem assessment process. Suppose that you want to assess the emotional maturity of a 6-year-old. According to developmental theorists (Bretherton, Fritz, Zahn-Waxler, & Ridgeway, 1986), 4– to 6-year-olds can identify basic feelings accurately and can communicate about simple emotions, but do not realize that feelings can be disguised or that different feelings can be experienced simultaneously. Based on this information, a board game could be constructed on a sheet of tagboard by drawing small squares at random on the board. Each square would have a number from 1 to 5 below it, and a face with a feeling (happy, sad, worried, mad, confused, very angry, excited) inside it. The child rolls the dice and moves his or her marker to a picture with that number under it, tries to identify the feeling, and talks about a time when he or she felt that way. Based on the child's responses, the practitioner will gain a sense of whether the child is experiencing a normal rate of emotional maturity.

Art Activities

Art activities often appeal to children and adolescents and are an excellent source of information regarding their perceptions and feelings about situations and aspects of their development. Limited only by one's creativity, the practitioner can involve young clients in drawing cartoons, self-portraits, family drawings, life-line murals, feeling collages, or doing clay sculptures or finger paint activities. Because they are easily administered, brief, and relatively nonthreatening, Oster and Gould (1987) advocated using art to learn more about the child to develop therapeutic goals. Koppitz (1983) cautioned that although activities of this nature are invaluable as part of an assessment procedure, they should be used in combination with other instruments, observations, and developmental background information.

Photography also can be used effectively to determine client self-perceptions. As noted by Harter and Pike (1984), self-understanding progresses from the concrete to abstract. Therefore, if asking an adolescent to look at a photograph of him or herself, the practitioner might expect that the youth would be able to describe him or herself based not only on physical appearance, but also descriptions based on values, beliefs, and dispositions. Comparing the responses to theories of self-development provides information that can be used to structure interventions.

Storytelling and Bibliotherapy

Literature serves a variety of purposes in counseling, and can be used effectively in the assessment process by providing young clients, particularly those who like to read, with fiction or nonfiction that presents issues similar to those that they might be dealing with at their stage of development (Shrank, 1982). Bibliotherapy is especially helpful with clients who are reluctant to express their thoughts and feelings. Having a structure such as the reading material to rely on facilitates discussion of issues they may be experiencing. Assigning *The Diary of Anne Frank* (Frank, 1963) to an adolescent girl is an effective way to assess feelings and concerns about puberty, for example. Reading and discussing *Where the Wild Things Are* (Sendak, 1963) to a first grader provides information about this child's fear and fantasies. Based on developmental theory, the practitioner knows that fear of the dark and fantasy are typical at this stage of development (Merritt, 1991), and can compare the child's responses to this information to determine the degree of concern and level of intervention.

Preschool children benefit from Gardner's (1971) mutual storytelling technique. With this approach, the counselor and the child tell a story. The counselor begins it with phrases that parallel the child's situation and then has the child tell the story. Used as an assessment device, this procedure is an effective way to determine what the child is thinking or feeling about a situation. Comparing data to developmental patterns assists the practitioner in designing appropriate interventions if needed.

Self-Monitoring

Self-monitoring techniques are helpful in determining the degree to which a child or adolescent is experiencing a particular feeling, behavior, or concern. These techniques can assume a variety of formats and are easy to use.

1. Feeling charts: clients draw a feeling face or write a feeling to represent how they feel at different points throughout the day. This gives good baseline data for determining depression.
2. Worry boxes: clients write worries on small sheets of paper and put them in the worry box. The counselor and clients discuss them to determine the extent of the worries, how they compare to developmental concerns, and where to intervene.

3. Food, exercise charts: clients keep a record of food and exercise to assess eating habits/eating disorders.
4. Temper/behavior graphs: clients monitor their temper tantrums, aggressive or nonassertive behavior, and bullying or cooperative behavior by doing daily charting.

Role-Play Activities

Given the limited verbal ability of some children, role playing can be used as an assessment device for various kinds of problems. The role-play technique engages the client and counselor in acting out a situation or dilemma. Based on the child's responses, the counselor can ascertain the problematic areas more clearly. To structure the role play, select the topic and invite the child to participate: "Let's act out this problem with your friends so that I have a better idea about what's bothering you. I'll be your friend, and you be yourself. Why don't you start and pretend that we're on the playground since that's where you said the problems happen. What happens?" The practitioner can refer to Selman's (1980) stages of interpersonal development, which illustrate the developmental stages, and then compare the client's responses to determine developmental level and target areas for intervention.

Play Therapy

Play therapy has been recognized as an exceptionally valuable means of learning about children (Landreth, 1987; Schaefer, 1985). Used as part of the assessment process, play becomes the medium to communicate concerns and express emotional issues. Dolls, puppets, or family figurines provide insight about family dynamics and physical or sexual abuse. A "magic wand" illustrates fantasies, worries, or wishes. Dress-up clothes can yield information about gender-role awareness, family interaction and roles, and social play and development issues. Using these data in conjunction with developmental norms helps the practitioner understand the level of concern.

DEVELOPMENTAL ASSESSMENT INSTRUMENTS

It is critical for professionals to know what type of information can be gained from various assessment techniques and instruments. As Garbarino and Stott (1989) noted, a clear conceptualization of the purpose of the assessment helps determine whether a test is the best method for gathering the information. In many instances, the what and how of assessment is a judgment call of the practitioner. For instance, if you were assessing acting out behavior, you probably would get a more accurate perspective from the teacher or parent. On the other hand, if you wanted to know how depressed a child was, asking the parent alone would be insufficient. A comprehensive assessment generally will include both formal and informal assessment techniques, with information obtained from multiple sources.

Developmental tests or screening instruments often are given to infants, toddlers, and preschoolers to assess developmental status. The *Bayley Scales of Infant Development* (Bayley, 1969) and the *McCarthy Scales of Children's Abilities* (McCarthy, 1972) are well-known examples of this type of assessment. Garbarino and Stott (1989) indicated that, although these tests are useful for assessing cognitive delay, they do not predict later cognitive abilities, and therefore should be considered only descriptive of current developmental status. Fraiberg (1980) contended that developmental tests often fail to assess social and emotional functioning comprehensively, and noted that testing is not the best method for learning about the child's ability to interact and form relationships. According to this author, direct observation in structured and unstructured settings is the best way to collect this type of data.

In the emotional area as well, practitioners rely heavily on structured and unstructured observations and interviews with significant adults in the child's life, rather than on a formal test. Recently, Greenspan (1979, 1981), Greenspan and Lieberman (1980), and Greespan and Porges (1984) developed a procedure for assessing emotional functioning in young children. By integrating developmental theory and information from clinical case studies, Greenspan formulated the clinical developmental structuralist approach to assessment and diagnosis. Through this approach, it is possible to determine whether the child has completed tasks at each developmental level and whether the emotional patterns are adaptive or maladaptive. The reader is referred to the entire issue of *Psychological Issues* (Greenspan, 1979) for further information.

Developmental assessment instruments usually are used to assess both biologically based and socially developed skills, and provide an evaluation of a child's cognitive, socioemotional, language, and motor abilities (Garbarino & Stott, 1989; Goldman, Stein, & Guerry, 1983). Some authors, such as Garbarino and Stott, distinguished between developmental screening tests and developmental assessment tests. They noted the purpose of developmental screening is prevention through early intervention, whereas developmental assessment tests provide a more comprehensive evaluation that results in a diagnosis from which recommendations can be made. In either case, this type of assessment can be used to help identify how normally children are developing or in what ways they are not. With this information, prevention, intervention, or appropriate placement can be determined.

The following list identifies examples of developmental assessment instruments appropriate for use with children and adolescents.

Physiological System Survey

Developed by Fadely and Hosler (1980), this extensive checklist identifies developmental characteristics for children from ages 2 to 5 in several different dimensions: physical, social, personality, cognitive, language, sensory motor, auditory perceptual, visual perceptual, and psychosocial development.

Questions such as the following are used to identify developmental progression:

Social Development (3 years)
___ Begins to wait for turn
___ Distinguishes between boys and girls
___ Loves to be with other children
___ Does not share willingly
Social Development (4–5 years)
___ Swearing and silly words
___ Imagination varied and vivid
___ Endless questions of how and why
___ Cooperative play with rapid change in friends
Language, Personality, and Cognitive Development (3 years)
___ Begins to show self-control
___ Temper tantrums at a peak
___ Enjoys praise
___ Imaginary worries; fears dark, dogs, death
Language, Personality, and Cognitive Development (4–5 years)
___ Name calling added to tantrums
___ Acts out if he or she does not get his or her way
___ Boastful, dogmatic, bossy
___ Difficulty in separation of fantasies and reality

The complete checklist can be found in *Developmental Psychometrics: A Resourcebook for Mental Health Workers and Educators* (From Fadely & Hosler, 1980, courtesy of Charles C Thomas, Publisher, Springfield, Illinois).

Washington University Sentence Completion Test

Developed by Loevinger, Wessler, and Redmore (1978) to assess stages of ego-development, this paper-and-pencil test consists of 36 unfinished sentences and can be completed in 30–45 minutes. The responses to the items are matched with those listed in *Measuring Ego Development II* by Loevinger et al. (1978). Other unfinished sentence tests for young-sters are the Rotter Incomplete Sentence Blank (Rotter & Rafferty, 1950) and the Hart Sentence Completion Test for Children (Hart, 1972).

Developmental Profile

Five areas of development are measured in this test developed by Alpern, Boll, and Shearer (1980): physical development, self-help capability, social development, academic development, and communi-cation. This test is appropriate for children from birth to age 12.

Bender Visual-Motor Gestalt Test for Children (Bender, undated)

Generally administered to children between ages 5 and 10, this test is used to indicate personality, organicity, and emotional maturity. The test consists of sample designs that are presented one at a time on cards. The child is asked to reproduce these card designs.

Goodenough-Harris Drawing Test

Accuracy of observation and conceptual thinking ability are emphasized in this test developed by Harris (1963). The test, which can be administered to clients from 3 to 15 years in age, assesses perceptual speed and accuracy, spatial aptitude, and reasoning. Originally known as the Draw-A-Man Test, it consists of drawing three figures—a man, a woman, and a self-portrait. The child is asked to draw the figures as completely as possible, and there are no time constraints. The scoring manual describes how credits are given to such factors as inclusion of body parts, detail, and accuracy of proportions of the figures. Based on the scores, an estimate of intellectual ability is derived.

Personal Orientation Inventory

This instrument was developed by Shostron (undated) and can be used for self-awareness for high school students and adults. It is based on Abraham Maslow's Hierarchy of Needs. There are 150 questions that yield 12 scores: time competence, inner directedness, self-actualizing value, existentiality, feeling reactivity, spontaneity, self-regard, self-acceptance, nature of man, synergy, acceptance of aggression, and capacity for intimate contact.

Vineland Social Maturity Scale

This instrument (Doll, 1965) can be used with individuals of all ages. The items measure developmental maturation in self-help, self-direction, locomotion, occupation, communication, and social relations.

Social Recognition Skills Checklist

This checklist, developed by Fadely and Hosler (1980), consists of 25 specific areas of social abilities that provide an extensive amount of information. Questions such as these are rated on a 1–10 scale:

1. Rights of others—awareness and acceptance of the rights of other people as distinct from the child's: (a) Does your child respect the ownership of toys and objects by others? Does your child ask permission to play with them rather than merely taking them? (b) Does your child accept and abide by the rules at school and home designed for group management?
2. Empathy—the awareness of the feelings of others and a willingness to attempt to understand their needs: (a) Does your child display appropriate concern and feelings of understanding toward situations and events that affect others? (b) Does your child feel the happiness and pain of others with true empathy followed by comforting behaviors?

Other dimensions addressed include internalization of social values, expressiveness, assertiveness, listening skills, leadership, cooperation, and altruism. The complete checklist can be found in *Developmental Psychometrics: A Resourcebook for Mental Health Workers and Educators* (Fadely & Hosler, 1980).

16 Personality Factors for Adolescents

This test, developed by Cattell, Eber, and Tatsuoka (1970), is an objective assessment of personality characteristics. There is also a children's version called the Children's Personality Questionnaire (CSQ), which includes two forms: the Early School Personality Questionnaire (ESPQ), for young children ages 6–8, and the High School Personality Questionnaire (HSPQ). Sample factors in these tests include: reserved or outgoing personality characteristics, identification of cognitive style, stability and emotional maturity factors, inactive versus overactive behavior, and social dependence versus self-sufficient behavior.

The Denver Developmental Screening Test and the Developmental Profile

These screening tools, developed by Frankenburg, Dodd, and Fandal (1973), are designed to identify developmental delays. There are 105 test items that assess personal/social (interpersonal and self-help behaviors), fine-motor (eye-hand coordination), language (receptive and expressive), and gross motor (sitting, walking, jumping) abilities. The Denver is used with children from birth to 6 years of age, and the newer Profile can be used with beginning adolescence to assess developmental change.

Purdue Perceptual-Motor Survey (PPMS)

This test was produced by Roach and Kephart (1966) and provides teachers with a means to identify children in first through fourth grades who may lack perceptual-motor skills needed for normal acquisition of academic skills. There are 22 items that cover laterality, directionality, and perceptual-motor matching.

Minnesota Child Development Inventory

The Minnesota Child Development Inventory (MCDI; Ireton & Thwing, 1979) is intended to be a supplementary measure and yields information about the developmental level of the child ages 1–6. There are 320 items about observable child behaviors, grouped into eight scales: general development, gross motor, fine motor, expressive language, situational and conceptual comprehension, self-help, and personal-social. It is to be completed by the mother.

Self-Concept Questionnaire

This checklist, designed by Fadely and Hosler (1980), is intended for use with both parents and children. Questions can be adapted so that it is appropriate for adolescents as well. The checklist consists of 20 items that assess physical, conceptual, affective, and social/value dimensions. The list should be given first to the parents and then to the child. The authors stress that the questions can be rephrased so that the child can respond at his or her comprehension level. Once both parent(s) and child have completed the checklist, it also should be given to a teacher or another adult who is very familiar with the child. Responses from all three persons can be compared to see where discrepancies occur. Sample questions to be rated on a 1–10 scale include:

1. Is the child physically attractive?
2. Does the child display adequate stamina, endurance?

3. Does the child speak and communicate adequately?
4. Does the child display average learning skills?
5. Does the child display appropriate emotional responses?
6. Does the child recover easily from disappointment or frustration?
7. Does the child recognize appropriate social behaviors in groups?
8. Does the display adequate cooperative behaviors with others?

These authors stress that the child's responses can be verified with behavioral observation in addition to the parent and teacher reports.

For the most part, all of the instruments described must be given by persons with considerable experience in test administration and scoring. The goal is to determine where children are relative to developmental milestones.

INTERVIEWING TECHNIQUES

Interviewing is an important way to learn about children, and even young children can share helpful perspectives of their own experiences and perceptions. However, children have various levels of cognitive understanding and verbal ability, and this must be taken into consideration to make the process worthwhile.

Adults need to avoid asking questions that go beyond children's abilities to respond. Garbarino and Stott (1989) cautioned that young school-aged children are sensitive to what they perceive as adult expectations, and may respond to these regardless of whether they have real information. Children younger than age 10 are less likely to know what they do or do not know.

In conducting interviews with children, it is important to take extra care that the child fully understands what is being asked and to rely on communication methods familiar to the child.

Questions asked during an interview must be appropriate to the child's developmental level. The following suggestions (Boat & Everson, 1989) may be helpful:

1. Rephrase, rather than repeat, questions the child does not understand.
2. Avoid asking questions that involve time sequence.
3. Use names instead of pronouns.
4. Try to use terms the child would use.
5. Acknowledge comments, but do not respond to every answer with another question.
6. Avoid long sentences.
7. Refer to familiar routines to stimulate recall.

8. Ask the child to repeat what you have said, rather than ask, "Do you understand?"
9. Use caution in interpreting responses to specific questions; children can be very literal.

Using props such as dolls, toy telephones, or human figures also can facilitate discussion during an interview.

Ivey (1986) created a model for assessing client developmental level during the interview process and matching counseling interventions with client needs. Ivey's model is an extension of Piagetian theory, but he stressed that clients represent a mixture of several developmental levels, although one usually predominates in the interview session. Ivey described the following as characteristic of lower developmental levels: incongruous verbal and nonverbal behaviors; negative "I" statements; negative, confused, and inappropriate emotions; passive and negative descriptors; external locus of control; and dependence or excessive independence. Conversely, higher developmental levels are characterized by congruent verbal and nonverbal behavior; positive "I" statements; positive emotions that are contextually appropriate; ability to deal with mixed feelings; active, positive descriptors; internal locus of control; and interdependence.

To assess cognitive functioning, Ivey (1986) suggested the following questions, adapted from Weinstein and Alschuler (1985):

1. Preoperational stage: Where did it happen? When? What were you doing? What did you do? How did you look?
2. Middle concrete operations stage: What were you feeling? What were you saying to yourself during this time? What did you think would happen?
3. Early formal operations stage: How did your response remind you of other situations? Is this a pattern? Do you feel the same way in other situations?
4. Late formal operations stage: When you feel that way, can you do anything about it? What could you do or say to yourself that would change what you are feeling or thinking? (p. 23)

It is apparent that higher levels of thinking are characterized by more emphasis on feelings and abstract thinking. Ivey (1986) suggested that these questions can assess developmental level, but also pointed out that clients are a mixture of several levels, depending on the topic. Careful attention to the clients' nonverbal behavior will assist the interviewer in determining level, as will attention to the characteristics of lower and higher developmental levels.

Shifting the interview style to meet developmental needs as described enhances the effectiveness of the assessment process, providing the practitioner with information that can be used to structure appropriate interventions that match developmental level.

A COMPREHENSIVE ASSESSMENT MODEL

Increased emphasis is placed on utilizing a variety of assessment approaches with children and adolescents to form a comprehensive picture of developmental progress and to target areas for intervention or prevention (Fadely & Hosler, 1980; Garbarino & Stott, 1989; Powell, 1981). Likewise, there is a trend toward mutual participation in the assessment and problem-solving process: involvement of the child, practitioner, and significant other adults.

One model of counseling that includes a multiple assessment focus, as well as mutual participation, is the BASIC ID, a multimodal approach developed by Lazurus (1976) and applied to children by Keat (1979). The BASIC ID is an acronym for behavior, affect, sensation, imagery, cognition, interpersonal relationships, and drugs/biology. The HELPING model, adapted for children from the BASIC ID (Keat, 1979), includes the following dimensions: (H)health, (E)emotions, (L)learning, (P)personal relationships, (I)imagery, (N)need to know, and (G)guidance of actions, behaviors, and consequences. As assessment models, both emphasize a holistic approach that helps the practitioner organize what is known about the young client and subsequently design appropriate developmental interventions to address areas that need strengthening.

The comprehensive nature of these models is particularly important, because it is easy to overlook a dimension of a problem during assessment. It is often this missing piece that sheds light on the real issue, as in the case of Darren.

Darren, a third grader, was brought to the attention of the counselor by his teacher who was concerned about his aggressive behaviors, which were most evident in his destruction of property. After the counselor interviewed Darren and discussed the problem with the teacher and parents, they agreed to try some behavior modification techniques to address the situation, because the problem did not seem to be emanating from excessive anger, poor peer or parental relationships, or academic frustration. However, after a period of time, it was apparent that the situation was not getting better. Particularly after lunch, Darren became rather hyperactive, carving on the desk with his pencil, tearing pages out of books, or kicking things out of his way. One day, after a discussion with the school nurse, the counselor asked Darren what he usually ate for lunch. "Jelly sandwiches and candy bars" was his reply. Some stories do have happy endings. In this case, once his parents started packing a more nutritious lunch, the behavior subsided. Had the counselor systematically assessed all areas of development, including health issues, this dimension would not have been ignored inadvertently.

The models presented by Ivey and Lazarus both addressed dimensions critical to child development and provided an effective means of targeting developmental concerns. A variety of both formal and informal assessment approaches can be used in conjunction with these models. The helping professional can ask directed, developmentally appropriate interview questions, make use of art or play mediums that may appeal to children who are kinesthetic learners, or design checklists or use commercially produced tests to determine specific areas of concern. The following case study illustrates this approach.

HELPING Assessment with Jesse

Jesse, a fourth grader, presented several concerns to the counselor. First of all, she worried about car accidents, bad storms and tornados, and fires. In addition, she and her 12-year-old brother did not get along at all. Jesse's parents questioned her frequent minor illnesses and school absences as a result.

In applying the HELPING model, first determine what you already know or infer about each dimension. In Jesse's case:

> *Health:* Frequent minor illnesses and school absences;
> *Emotions:* Anxiety about events related to natural disaster;
> *Learning:* Possibly behind in school due to absences;
> *Personal relationships:* Conflict with brother;
> *Imagery:* Seems to see self as powerless;
> *Need to know:* How to overcome helplessness; how to deal more directly with issues, rather than through avoidance (illness); and
> *Guidance of actions, behaviors, consequences:* Lacks conflict resolution strategies; exhibits avoidance (school) behavior.

After this initial overview, the practitioner decides what additional data need to be collected to get a comprehensive view of the problem(s). With a child this age, it is logical to involve the parent(s), who can provide information about when these problems began, how frequently she experiences the anxiety and school avoidance behavior, whether she has had a physical exam and the results, and more about the specifics of the relationship with her brother. You also would want to interview the teacher to learn more about the effect of her absences on her academic performance and if there seems to be any pattern to the absences. Checklists could be developed to get a more concrete representation of these data.

In interviewing Jesse, we know that as a 9-year-old she is probably in the concrete operations stage of cognitive development, and therefore is capable of more logical thought patterns. She also is able to anticipate and explain cause and effect, and can, to some extent, assume the viewpoint of others (Ivey, 1986). Drawing from Ivey's work, the following kinds of questions should be appropriate for Jesse; if not, she may be operating at a lower cognitive level and the focus would need to shift.

Counselor: "Jesse, you mentioned that you are afraid that something bad might happen to your family, like a tornado that would rip your house apart or a bad car accident. When you think about those things, what feelings do you have? Can you tell me some of the things that you say to yourself when you get scared like that?"

To further assess her anxiety, you could have her draw a picture of what she thinks might happen in these events and keep a chart that shows how often she gets anxious.

To evaluate the conflict with her brother, which is a relatively normal developmental issue, Jesse could be asked to keep a list of the different events that trigger the conflict, how often it occurs, and to rate it on a 1–5 scale in terms of intensity. Role playing also would be helpful in demonstrating the nature of the conflict and how each party reacted.

When the information from all sources has been gathered, it can be evaluated for patterns, specific problems, areas that may need to be assessed further, and areas of strength. A multimodal approach does not assume that there are problems in every dimension. But by identifying strengths or deficits in each area, a comprehensive assessment occurs. Following the assessment, specific interventions can be targeted for each area as needed. As with the assessment process, interventions may engage parents, siblings, teachers, or other school personnel in addition to counselor-directed strategies with the child.

SUMMARY

Childhood and adolescence are the formative periods when change is most dramatic. Helping professionals are frequently asked, "Is my child doing o.k.?" Children and adolescents express concern . . . "Am I normal?" These questions only can be answered by accurate assessment of the problem that utilizes a multifaceted approach, including information from a variety of sources.

As a young client in her 8-year-old wisdom stated, "I know my friend is sad and I want to help her, but unless she tells me what's wrong, I don't know what to do." This is the concept of assessment. Until more is known about the problem and how it interfaces with developmental stages, intervention cannot be determined. Given that one in five American children has a developmental, learning, or emotional problem, according to the 1988 National Health Interview Study of Child Health (Drummond, 1992), it appears that helping professionals need to take the concept of developmental assessment seriously.

REFERENCES

Alpern, G., Boll, T., & Shearer, M. (1980). *Developmental profile II.* Aspen, CO: Psychological Development Publications.
Bayley, N. (1969). *The bayley scales of infant development.* New York: The Psychological Corporation.
Bender, L. (n.d.). *Bender visual motor gestalt test for children.* Beverly Hills, CA: Western Psychological Services.
Boat, B. W., & Everson, M. D. (1989). The anatomical doll project: An overview. In J. Garbarino & F. Stott (Eds.), *What children can tell us* (pp. 170–202). San Francisco, CA: Jossey-Bass.
Bradley, L. (1988). Developmental assessment: A life-span approach. In R. Hayes & R. Aubrey (Eds.), *New directions for counseling and human development* (pp. 136–157). Denver, CO: Love.
Bretherton, I., Fritz, J., Zahn-Waxler, C., & Ridgeway, D. (1986). Learning to talk about emotions: A functionalist perspective. *Child Development, 57,* 529–548.
Cattell, R. B., Eber, H. W., & Tatsuoka, M. M. (1970). *Handbook for the 16 personality factor questionnaire.* Champaign, IL: Institute for Personality and Ability Testing.
Doll, E. (1965). *Vineland social maturity scale.* Circle Pines, MN: American Guidance Service.
Drummond, R. (1992). *Appraisal procedures for counselors and helping professionals.* New York: Merrill.
Fadely, J., & Hosler, V. (1980). *Developmental psychometrics: A resourcebook for mental health workers and educators.* Springfield, IL: Charles C. Thomas.
Fraiberg, S. (Ed.). (1980). *Clinical studies in infant mental health.* New York: Basic Books.
Frank, A. (1963). *The diary of Anne Frank.* New York: Washington Square Press.
Frankenburg, W. K., Dodd, J. B., & Fandal, A. W. (1973). *Denver developmental screening test.* Denver, CO: Ladora Project and Publishing.
Garbarino, J., & Stott, F. (1989). *What children can tell us.* San Francisco, CA: Jossey-Bass.
Gardner, R. A. (1971). *Therapeutic communication with children: The mutual storytelling technique in child psychotherapy.* New York: Aronson.

Goldman, J., Stein, C., & Guerry, S. (1983). *Psychological methods of child assessment.* New York: Brunner/Mazel.

Greenspan, S. I. (1979). Intelligence and adaptation: An integration of psychoanalytic and piagetian developmental psychology [Special Issue]. *Psychological Issues, 47–48.*

Greenspan, S. I. (1981). *Psychopathology and adaptation in infancy and early childhood: Principles of clinical diagnoses and preventive intervention.* New York: International Universities Press.

Greenspan, S. I., & Lieberman, A. F. (1980). Infants, mothers, and their interaction: A quantitative clinical approach to developmental assessment. In S. I. Greenspan & G. H. Pollock (Eds.), *The course of life: Psychoanalytic contributions toward understanding personality development* [Special Issue] (Vol. 1). Washington, DC: U.S. Government Printing Office.

Greenspan, S. I., & Porges, S. W. (1984). Psychopathology in infancy and early childhood: Clinical perspectives on the organization of sensory and affective-thematic experience. *Child Development, 55,* 49–70.

Guidubaldi, J., DeZolt, D., & Myers, M. A. (1991). Assessment and diagnostic services for prekindergarten children. *Elementary School Guidance and Counseling, 26,* 45-56.

Harris, D. (1963). *Children's drawings as a measure of intellectual maturity.* Orlando, FL: Harcourt Brace Jovanovich.

Hart, D. H. (1972). *The hart sentence completion test for children.* Unpublished manuscript. Salt Lake City, UT: Educational Support Systems.

Harter, S. (1988). Developmental processes in the construction of the self. In T. D. Yawkey & J. E. Johnson (Eds.), *Integrative processes and socialization: Early to middle childhood* (pp. 45–78). Hillsdale, NJ: Lawrence Erlbaum Associates.

Harter, S., & Pike, R. (1984). The pictoral scale of perceived competence and social acceptance for young children. *Child Development, 55,* 1969–1982.

Ireton, E., & Thwing, E. (1979). *Minnesota child development inventory.* Minneapolis, MN: Behavior Systems.

Ivey, A. (1986). *Developmental therapy.* San Francisco, CA: Jossey-Bass.

Keat, D. L. (1979). *Multimodal therapy with children.* New York: Pergamon.

Kohlberg, L. (1981). *The philosophy of moral development.* New York: Harper & Row.

Koppitz, E. M. (1983). Projective drawings with children and adolescents. *School Psychology Review, 12,* 421–427.

Landreth, G. (1987). Play therapy: Facilitative use of child's play in elementary school counseling. *Elementary School Guidance and Counseling, 21,* 253–261.

Lazurus, A. A. (1976). *Multimodal behavior therapy.* New York: Springer.

Loevinger, J., Wessler, R., & Redmore, C. (1978). *Measuring ego development* (Vols. 1 & 2). San Francisco, CA: Jossey-Bass.

McCarthy, D. (1972). *McCarthy scales of children's abilities.* New York: The Psychological Corporation.

Merritt, J. E. (1991). Reducing a child's nighttime fears. *Elementary School Guidance and Counseling, 25,* 291–295.

Oster, G. D., & Gould, P. (1987). *Using drawings in assessment and therapy: A guide for mental health professionals.* New York: Bruner/Mazel.

Powell, M. (1981). *Assessment and management of developmental changes and problems in children.* St. Louis, MO: C.V. Mosby.

Roach, E. F., & Kephart, N. C. (1966). *Purdue perceptual motor survey.* Columbus, OH: Merrill.

Rotter, J. B., & Rafferty, J. E. (1950). *Manual for the rotter incomplete sentence blank.* New York: Psychological Corporation.

Santrock, J., & Yussen, S. R. (1992). *Child development: An introduction.* Dubuque, IA: William C. Brown.

Schaefer, C. E. (1985). Play therapy. *Early Child Development and Care, 19,* 95–108.

Selman, R. (1980). *The growth of interpersonal understanding: Developmental and clinical analyses.* New York: Academic Press.

Selman, R. (1981). The child as a friendship philosopher. In S. R. Asher & J. M. Gottman (Eds.), *The development of children's friendships* (pp. 242–272). New York: Academic Press.

Sendak, M. (1963). *Where the wild things are.* New York: Harper.

Shostron, E. (n.d). *Personal orientation inventory.* San Diego, CA: Educational and Industrial Testing Service.

Shrank, F. (1982). Bibliotherapy as an elementary school counseling tool. *Elementary School Guidance and Counseling, 16,* 218-227.

Weinstein, G., & Alschuler, A. (1985). Education and counseling for self-knowledge development. *Journal of Counseling and Development, 64,* 19-25.

Yussen, S. R. (1977). Characteristics of moral dilemmas written by adolescents. *Developmental Psychology, 13,* 162-163.

CHAPTER III

DESIGNING DEVELOPMENTAL INTERVENTIONS

Several counseling students were discussing a case study during practicum class. "I just wish there was a recipe to follow so that I would know exactly what to do, how, and when," said Sue. "I always wonder if I'm doing the right thing, and sometimes I can't even think of an intervention." Sound familiar? On the down side, it is frustrating when you cannot come up with the right intervention; on the other hand, this is where the counseling process is a challenging and creative endeavor.

Although there is no recipe as such, the purpose of this chapter is to share some specific information that will assist in the intervention phase of the counseling process. A four-stage process for designing interventions is outlined, including specific considerations in designing developmentally appropriate interventions. Examples of a wide variety of interventions that are particularly applicable for school-aged children also are described.

THE DESIGN PROCESS

Counseling with children and adolescents must not be a "fly by the seat of your pants" endeavor. Interventions must be developed and selected after careful consideration, taking into account the developmental level of the child, how he or she assimilates concepts, time constraints, and the appropriateness of the method for the particular problem.

In designing an effective intervention, both the counselor and client need a sense of direction and purpose that can be achieved through a planned change process (Reynolds, 1993). Adapted from Reynolds' model, four stages integral to this process are described subsequently: planning, design of intervention, implementation, and evaluation.

Planning Stage

Following problem assessment, in which the presenting concern is explored in detail to determine when it began, under what conditions it occurs, and with what degree of frequency and intensity, the counselor and client can proceed to the planning stage of the intervention design process. This stage consists of the following six substages:

1. Vision: Compared to how things are now, what could be different? How could things be better? What would be ideal?
2. Goal setting: What is going well? What needs to be worked on? What are the goals for change?
3. Analysis: What is enabling or interfering with achieving these goals or this vision? What is getting in the way of resolving the problem?
4. Objective: What specifically would the client (or the parent or the teacher) like to change? The objective should be stated measurably, such as "to identify five ways to control anger."
5. Exploration of interventions: What already has been tried and how did it work? How does the client learn best? Where is the child relative to developmental stages? Will parents or significant others be involved in the process? What research has been done on the most effective types of interventions for this specific problem? What is the counselor's skill level relative to design and implementation of various interventions?

Designing the Intervention

Rather than prescribe an intervention, it generally is more effective to collaborate as much as possible with the young client and parents as appropriate in the intervention design process. Not only does this reduce resistance, but frequently clients or significant others can contribute ideas that increase the effectiveness of the particular intervention and, in turn, the likelihood that it will be successful. I recall working with 4-year-old Nick, a bright and verbal youngster who was aggressive and impulsive with peers as well as adults. Although I had identified several interventions after a thorough assessment of the problem, I met with his parents to solicit their input as to what might be most effective, because they also would be working with him during the implementation stage. As I shared some ideas with role playing, his father indicated that Nick liked to play dress up, and that one of his favorite activities was to accompany his dad to the community theater when Dad was rehearsing for a play because he liked to try on costumes. Through brainstorming, we developed some specific interventions, using dress-up clothes to act out appropriate and inappropriate behaviors in different situations with different people. Had I not involved the parents, I would not have had the information needed to personalize an intervention to increase its applicability.

The following guidelines should be useful in designing and selecting developmentally appropriate interventions for children and adolescents.

1. Children's thinking progresses from concrete to abstract; use concrete analogies, props, pictures, and drawings as part of the intervention with young clients. Example: "We've talked about how you feel and what you can do when someone calls you a name. Now, if you could draw a picture of a solution in each of these squares, you can tape it to your desk to help remind you what you can do."

2. Younger children's attention spans are more limited, so integrate the assessment/intervention process as much as possible, including a variety of approaches. Example: Counselor to 6-year-old Katya, "First I'd like you to draw a picture for me that shows that secret hiding place you have been talking about going to when you are scared. Then I'll read you a story about a little girl your age who gets scared like you do. Maybe you can get some ideas from the story about what helps her when she feels scared."

3. Children's ability to remember concepts from session to session may be limited. Making use of short homework assignments that reinforce or introduce interventions that the young client can be working on throughout the week is helpful. Example: "Jason, this week when you feel like you're so frustrated that you're ready to explode, try taking a deep breath and mentally picturing a big stop sign in front of your face. STOP stands for: Stop, Think, Overcome, and Progress."

4. Use concrete, simple explanations with children who are at the concrete operational stage of cognitive development. Demystify the counseling process so that it seems more like problem solving rather than analyzing. Example: Rather than saying, "Maria, you seem to have a problem with anxiety; let's see what we can do about that," phrase it as, "Maria, I understand that you are worried about how you'll get along in second grade. Would you be willing to make a list of the things you worry about and bring them next time? Then I can help you figure out some things you can do so that you won't have to worry as much."

5. Children and adolescents need to see a reason for counseling. Engaging them in a discussion of their goals and explaining how the particular intervention can help them achieve that goal is

important. Example: Tom, an 18-year-old, shared that his goal was to terminate a long-standing relationship with his girlfriend. The counselor explained concepts of assertive communication to him and invited him to role play effective communication skills that would help him explain his position more effectively to his girlfriend.

6. Younger clients learn best if interventions are specific and personal. Interview them about their interests, talents, heroes, favorite television shows, and rock groups, as well as how they like to learn. Use this information in structuring personalized interventions. Example: Ten-year-old Maggie loved to draw cartoons. One of the interventions used to help her develop more positive peer relationships was to have her make a cartoon book illustrating positive ways to maintain friendships.

7. Using relevant examples and interventions contributes to the effectiveness with adolescents. Invite them to share yearbooks and pictures of friends and relatives so that examples and interventions are meaningful. Example: After Carol shared her pictures from camp, the counselor utilized examples in her intervention. "Carol, you told me that you had a miserable time at camp and that you never did anything with anybody. But when I look at this picture that shows you and Susie and Liz laughing as you are canoeing together, I wonder if maybe you did have some fun after all? Do you think that you might have been overgeneralizing just a bit about this experience? Let's backtrack and make a list of specifically what was good, what was terrible, and what was awful. Maybe that will give you a different perspective."

8. Children and adolescents retain concepts more readily if they are involved in selecting meaningful analogies, activities, and interventions. Example: Nine-year-old Phillip got frustrated easily when he couldn't do things right. He and the counselor worked on some self-statements that he could use in these situations, and the counselor asked him if he could think of something that would help him remember not to get so upset and to use his self-statements. She shared an example with him that an older boy had used for a similar problem. He had pretended that his head was a giant bug zapper and that those frustrating thoughts would just be "fried" before they got inside his head. Phillip said that he would pretend that his head was a giant eraser and he could just erase the thoughts that caused his frustration.

9. It is critical to structure age-appropriate interventions. For instance, most adolescents are "wired" to their tape and compact disc players, and young children respond well to games. Example:

Invite adolescents to make a music collage, tape-recording segments of songs that they think illustrate positive ways for them to
solve their problems. With young children, make a game such as
Give a Little (Vernon, self-developed game), in which students roll
dice, move a given number of spaces, select a conflict card, and
identify effective conflict resolution strategies.

10. Consider the client's learning style. Although counseling traditionally has been characterized by a verbal orientation, Myrick (1987)
cautioned that some clients "may feel hopelessly inundated with
words when being 'counseled.' They may feel overwhelmed,
insecure, or lost in the intellectual efforts that seem to form the
basis of most school counseling and guidance" (p. 131). Rather
than limit the effectiveness of the intervention with clients whose
learning styles are not primarily auditory, a wide array of interventions that access a variety of learning styles should be considered:
art activities, drama and play, music and movement, games,
imagery, and bibliotherapy. Example: Seven-year-old Melinda
literally bounced off the walls during counseling sessions. Drama
and play interventions were more effective than verbal approaches
for a child with limited attention span and a tactual, kinesthetic
orientation.

11. The timing of an intervention is critical. Do not rush the process
or try to implement interventions that are too advanced for the
client at this stage in the counseling process. Example: Although
17-year-old Marcos wanted to begin dating, the counselor needed
to work with him to develop more self-confidence and overcome
his fear of rejection before encouraging him to ask out someone.
After this step, small interventions could be tried: talking to a
young woman on the school bus, calling her on the phone,
meeting after school for a soda, and, finally, asking her for a date.

12. What works with one child might not work with another, even if
it is the same problem. If an intervention does not work, swallow
your pride, and do not be afraid to try another. Counselors do not
have crystal balls and cannot always predict what will or will not
be effective. Although it is important to be on target as much as
possible, sometimes an intervention will not work because of the
client's readiness level or state of being at the time. Be flexible and
consider varying your approach. Example: A 14-year-old felt
inadequate in social situations. Previous interventions such as
assertive communication skills and self-concept activities had not
alleviated the problem. The counselor decided to obtain permission from this client to invite another teenager who also had had
similar problems to share with him his feelings and how he had

worked on the issues. This intervention was very effective; the client began to take more risks as he observed a peer modeling these behaviors to age-appropriate dilemmas.

13. Use language that is appropriate to the age of the child; rephrase as necessary. Learn their "lingo" to facilitate better communication. Example: To Tommy, age 6, "Could you draw me a picture that shows what you can do when you have your 'yucky' feelings at school?"

14. Develop a good rapport and a sense of trust with the child, adolescent, and significant others before designing an intervention that might be too threatening or too unusual. Example: Carla and her mother were constantly at odds, with Carla desperately trying to gain power and control of the relationship. Carla discovered that what really "got" to her mother was her foul mouth; and although this resulted in being grounded to the bathroom for various periods of time, it did not bother this 13-year-old. After meeting with the mother alone and explaining the obvious power struggle, the counselor invited the mother to try structuring a 10-minute swearing time each day. Once this was initiated, the swearing stopped, because, once again, mother was in control.

15. Have a good rationale for the selection of a given intervention. As stated previously, counseling is not a "fly by the seat of your pants" endeavor. There should be a clear connection between the assessed problem and the intervention. Example: Sharon does not know how to express her anger. Instead of focusing on this skill, the counselor had her discuss her strengths and weaknesses and make a *Me Badge* (Vernon, 1988). Although this certainly would be appropriate if the problem related to self-concept, with an issue as specific as expression of anger, the counselor can teach this skill more directly.

16. Do not be gimicky. In other words, do not use interventions because they may be appealing to the client or fun to try. There needs to be a reason for choosing the intervention. Example: Tony loves to play checkers, so he and the counselor play a game during each counseling session and chat about how things are going. Although this may be a good rapport builder, it does not address the assessed problem. It would be possible to adapt the checkers game by having Tony share ways to stay tuned to a task after a move if paying attention was his problem.

17. Do not overstructure. Beginning counselors have a tendency to rely on a specific plan that includes interventions for each counseling session. Although it is important to structure interventions based on the assessed problem, it also is important to have

latitude to go in a different direction if new information is presented. Do not lock yourself in. Example: In the previous session, Emily had completed an unfinished sentence checklist that indicated that she had some problems with her mother. The counselor selected a book to read to Emily, but Emily seemed distracted during the session and said that she needed to talk about her grade on a test. Allow some flexibility; remember that children sometimes have a problem one week, but it may be gone the next; judge accordingly.

Implementation Stage

After the intervention has been selected, the next stage is implementation. This stage occurs in several ways: (a) immediately following the design of the intervention, within the same session; (b) as a homework assignment for the client to implement between sessions; (c) as a "step-by-step" implementation, in which a segment of the intervention is worked on, followed by additional steps after successful completion of the first; and (d) a combination of all of these.

In working with younger clients, it is important to remember that, because their sense of time is so immediate, it may be necessary to identify one aspect of a problem, design an intervention, and move directly to implementation in a short period of time. The advantage of this approach is that it shows the children and their parents that something can be done, which makes the problem seem less overwhelming. The possible disadvantage is that the entire process is more piecemeal. However, as a 10-year-old once said, "I need help now! Maybe my friend won't be mad at me tomorrow, but I can't wait 'till then to make things better." Thus, one needs to consider with whom one is working and adapt the process accordingly. Furthermore, after this intervention has been selected and implemented, the counselor and client can recycle into further problem assessment and then reenter the planning stage to target another issue.

Furthermore, helping professionals must use their judgment to determine how much of the problem to address and at what pace to proceed with interventions. To some extent, this depends on the age of the client and on the magnitude and degree of intensity of the problem. If the problem interferes a lot with daily living and is causing a great deal of distress to the client or to others in the system, it is advisable to work on portions of the problem and intervene sooner, recycling back as necessary.

Interventions also can be implemented successfully as a homework assignment. Not only does this reinforce concepts discussed during the counseling session, but it also is particularly helpful for younger clients whose recall ability from session to session is often limited. Homework assignments can assume a variety of formats:

1. Reading: biographies, fiction, nonfiction, poetry, magazine or newspaper articles.
2. Writing: journals, diaries, poetry, fiction, letters to express emotions or clarify thoughts.
3. Behavioral tasks: risk-taking exercises, task completion, learning new skills.
4. Observing/viewing: specific movies, television programs, ways in which others behave or approach situations.

It is important to invite the young client to participate in the homework assignment. The counselor can explain the purpose of the task and how this will help the young client achieve identified goals.

Working on segments of an intervention also contributes to its effectiveness. For instance, with an anxious child, behavioral interventions need to be developed and implemented in a carefully structured hierarchy by breaking the ultimate goal into manageable steps appropriate to the child's developmental abilities. If too much is initiated too soon, the child may get discouraged and the entire procedure may fail. Although dividing the intervention into successive parts takes careful planning and patience, it is well worth the effort in the long run.

Evaluation

Did the intervention work? This is the key question to ask during the evaluation stage. Characteristically, when problems are not resolved, there has not been adequate evaluation to be tried. However, time constraints, lack of commitment, or lack of momentum often interfere with this critical step. The intervention may be implemented, and things may temporarily improve, but unless a systematic evaluative procedure is exercised, the implementation process is incomplete. Inevitably, without a deliberate assessment of what did or did not work, the problem increases in severity and intensity, which prompts the client or others to seek assistance again. Unfortunately, by allowing the problem to become more severe, subsequent change efforts become more difficult, as illustrated in the following case study.

Damien, age 10, saw his school counselor on several occasions for help in adjusting to a recent physical disability. After assessing the problem and identifying several interventions, Damien, his parents, and his teachers implemented the plan. During the first few weeks when the counselor and Damien discussed his progress, things were going well.

Damien's parents and teachers also confirmed this. However, as is frequently the case with school counselors, more immediate needs arose, and the counselor stopped seeing Damien on a regular basis. Not surprisingly, after a month, Damien's parents called the counselor to say he resisted going to school and had withdrawn from his friends in church and scouting activities. By this time, Damien was more depressed. He and the counselor started over again to determine what to do about the initial problem and these subsequent symptoms.

Naturally, it is not always possible to prevent a situation like this from occurring, given the nature of the problem and the reality that things sometimes get worse before they get better. However, ongoing evaluation and gradual termination are recommended as a means of avoiding this situation. Involving parents or teachers in the evaluative process also is critical, because too often a child is ready to say "everything's okay," when the teacher or parent sees little or no improvement. In Damien's case, after several weeks of progress, a short evaluation session with Damien, his parents, and teachers could have determined what had worked and what issues still needed to be addressed. A phase-out process could have been established to provide further evaluation and support. By considering evaluation an integral part of the intervention process, a feedback loop is established. That is, based on the evaluation, it may be necessary to recycle back to the planning stage, then to designing and implementing new strategies to address various aspects of the problem.

THE FOUR-STAGE DESIGN PROCESS: A CASE STUDY

The case of Sandra illustrates the application of this four-stage model. Sandra, a 13-year-old, was referred to the school counselor by her mother, because of her defiant behavior and low grades. During the assessment process, which included both Sandra and her mother at separate times, it was determined that this client was of above-average intelligence with several other problems: inferiority feelings and lack of friends, some experimentation with alcohol and tobacco, jealousy toward her baby sister, and rebellious actions and attitudes, which created frequent and intense conflict with her mother and her mother's live-in boyfriend.

Because there were several problems in this case, the counselor and client needed to agree during the planning stage about which problem to address first. In Sandra's opinion, the reason she was starting to drink, smoke, and get low grades was because she was angry at her mother and did not like Mom's boyfriend. Because she expressed her anger defiantly, which increased conflict between mother and daughter, the counselor agreed that this issue was of more immediate concern than the inferiority, friendship, and sibling issues.

During the planning stage, Sandra was asked about her vision: Compared to how things are now, how could they be different or better? She identified it would be better if they did not fight as much. Next, they discussed goals: What things were going well? Sandra was a pretty unhappy child and could not identify much that was going well. Her goals for change included to feel happier and get along better with her mother. Next, the counselor and Sandra discussed what was interfering with achieving the goals and resolving the problem. In her opinion, she would feel happier if Mom's boyfriend did not live with them, but admitted that they had had problems even before that had occurred. As Sandra described their conflicts, the counselor drew a circular pattern of interaction to help explain what happens when one person reacts to another: If Mom refused to let Sandra do what she wanted to do, Sandra yelled, cursed, and called her names, which made Mom angry and resulted in Sandra's being grounded, which in turn prompted Sandra to be more rebellious. In this way, it became clear to this young client that the way she and her mother responded to each other created more problems.

Next, specific objectives were identified: (a) to learn how to deal with anger in constructive, rather than destructive, ways; and (b) to establish a more positive relationship with her mother by utilizing positive communication techniques.

After exploring what Sandra had tried in relation to the targeted problem, the counselor was ready to design and implement interventions to address the first objective. Sensing that this client was tactual, the counselor invited her to beat a plastic bat on a pillow and verbalize what angered her. The counselor took notes so that Sandra could also see what she had expressed. He also encouraged her to keep a journal or use a tape recorder to identify how she had felt so that this could be discussed in the following session. Next, he adapted an activity, "Healthy/Unhealthy Expression" (Vernon, 1989a, p. 191), to help Sandra distinguish between positive and negative ways to express anger and to identify advantages and disadvantages of both kinds of expression. This was followed by an activity called "Chain Reactions" (Vernon, 1989b, p. 33), which illustrated the chain effect of negative emotions resulting in negative behaviors. Before addressing the second objective, the counselor and Sandra discussed results of a weekly log, in which the client recorded the number of times she felt angry and acted defiantly and the ways in which she had expressed anger positively. This was a concrete way to determine any progress.

To deal with the second objective, the counselor and Sandra read the book *The Mouse, Monster and Me* (Palmer, 1977), discussing the difference between assertive, aggressive, and nonassertive communication. They also role played, with Sandra assuming each of these communication styles in situations pertaining to issues with her mother and the boyfriend. Sandra read *The Nine Most Troublesome Teenage Problems and How to Solve Them* (Bauman, 1986) to learn more about handling anger and talking to parents. The counselor also involved her in several small-group counseling sessions with other teenagers about getting along with parents. When he felt Sandra was ready to apply what she had learned, he encouraged her to invite her mother in so they could work on goals for improved communication.

Meeting with the mother also became part of the evaluation session: Was there less conflict? Were they better able to discuss situations? Sandra also had kept a weekly log to monitor progress. After determining that things had improved, the counselor continued to meet with Sandra to address the other issues, gradually decreasing the number of visits. A final "check-up" session for evaluation was held with Sandra and her mother.

Progression through this four-stage implementation model is enhanced by a repertoire of various interventions as described in the following section.

TYPES OF INTERVENTIONS

Recently, we added another Golden Retriever puppy to our family. Whereas our previous Golden was mellow and required little obedience training, Tawney presents another story. We relabeled her behavior "spirited" and have used a variety of techniques to help her develop a calmer nature. It did not take us long to realize, however, that what worked with one dog will not necessarily work with another, and if one strategy flops, there is always another one to try. It is much the same with counseling interventions. What works with one client will not necessarily work with another, but there are always new things to try. In the following section, specific examples of "tried and true" interventions appropriate for use with children and adolescents are described. Although several of these categories already were described in the assessment section, their purpose here is different: the assessment process provides the information and the intervention addresses the problem. As is true with assessment instruments, interventions for a school-aged clientele cannot be scaled-down versions of what works with adults. Rather, careful consideration needs to be given to: (a) the age, gender, cultural background, and developmental level of the client; (b) the types of interventions that might be most meaningful and appropriate for this particular client; and (c) the intervention(s) that will yield the best results and lead to problem resolution.

Writing Activities

When using writing activities, consider whether these are an appropriate intervention for the client. For children who find writing laborious, or who are more auditory or kinesthetic in their learning styles, this may not be the best intervention. The following are examples of writing activities described in relation to a specific problem(s) to clarify the procedure.

Journaling. Journaling, either structured or unstructured, is a form of expressive writing that some clients find useful (Hutchins & Cole, 1986). Journaling is a good form of catharsis, and is an especially effective intervention to use with adolescents on such issues as self-awareness, relationship issues, values clarification, or decision making. If the journaling is unstructured, the counselor simply invites the young client to record thoughts and feelings that occurred during the week, suggesting that if he or she chooses, elements of the journal may be shared with the counselor. If the journaling is structured, the counselor provides a list of suggestions to guide the writing.

Mary, a 16-year-old, was invited to journal about her ambivalent feelings in a relationship. The following suggestions were offered:

When I'm with this person I usually feel _____.
What I like best about this person is _____.
What I like least about this person is _____.
When I think about ending the relationship I feel _____.
What I've learned most from this relationship is _____.

Clarification can come through journaling of this nature and can be followed with more specific interventions that address the concerns.

Stories. Writing personal stories with different endings is an effective way to make a decision when it's difficult to select an alternative. Clients of all ages can participate in this type of intervention, although the counselor most likely will serve as the scribe for younger clients. This strategy was used with Jeremy, a seventh grader whose parents had forbidden him to associate with two of his classmates. For Jeremy, writing the stories with different endings that anticipated consequences helped clarify his decision about whether to obey his parents.

Poetry. Whether reading or writing it, poetry is a way to express emotions, healing and identifying aspects of self (Gladding, 1987). Younger children may need poetic stems, such as "I used to . . . but now I . . . ," as well as an illustration to get them started (Gladding, 1987, p. 308). Writing poetry results in increased sensitivity and insight. I find this intervention to be especially helpful with depressed adolescent females. Usually they need no prompting; they've been using poetry as a way to express themselves on their own. In a supportive counseling relationship, the catharsis through poetry is one way to help the client feel better.

Autobiographies. Because the purpose of an autobiography is to reflect on one's life, this intervention is more limited and perhaps most appropriate for high school juniors or seniors. According to Gibson and Mitchell (1990), writing an autobiography "lets a person express what has been important in his or her life, emphasize likes and dislikes, identify values, describe interests and aspirations, acknowledge success and failures, and recall meaningful relationships" (p. 278).

Autobiographies generally are written one of two ways–describing a particular segment or aspect of one's life, such as school, family, or relationships; or writing a chronicle that covers all of one's life history (Hutchins & Cole, 1986). Once the client provides the written material, the counselor helps the client clarify the issues by asking questions, probing for feelings, confronting discrepancies in the writing, identifying specific concerns, and setting goals for change (Vernon, 1991).

This intervention was used with a high school senior who needed to, in her words, "pull together the pieces so that I know where I'm going." A life-line activity that directs the client to identify specific major events also can be incorporated into the autobiography.

Therapeutic fairy tale. Gladding (1992) described the therapeutic fairy tale as a means to help adolescents deal with problematic issues. Clients are asked to imagine a scene that is far away from the present in both time and space, to include a problem in the setting, and to identify a positive solution to the problem. They are given 6–10 minutes to write the story, beginning it with the standard fairy tale opening, "Once upon a time." Clients can learn about themselves by looking at the qualities of the characters, what contributed to the solution, and how the story was created.

Therapeutic Games

It goes without saying that games are appealing to children, in particular, but also to adolescents, depending on the specific activity. I prefer to develop games or use commercially produced materials that relate specifically to the particular problem areas being addressed. Not only is it more cost-effective to design games, but it is also a better way to specifically tailor the game to the problem. Several original games are described first, followed by a list of games that can be purchased.

Fact or belief? Students of all ages readily confuse facts with beliefs (assumptions) about a given situation. Unless children learn to distinguish between facts and beliefs, they frequently distort the reality of the situation, which may have negative ramifications. To develop this game, draw a "tic tac toe" configuration on a sheet of tagboard. Next, on strips of paper, develop samples of facts and beliefs/assumptions appropriate to the problem and the age of the child with whom you are working. Examples for a fourth grader who routinely gets caught up in friendship misunderstandings might include: Tanya is in my class; Tanya doesn't like me; if Susan sits by someone else, it means she hates me; there are nine girls in my section, and so on. The game is played like "tic tac toe"; each time the client makes a mark, he or she draws a strip and identifies it as a fact or belief. Discussion follows, with emphasis on how to check out assumptions as a way to clarify friendship issues.

Options. Designed to help with decision making, this game can be adapted for elementary and middle school students. Materials include a set of cards that contains decision-making dilemmas. Examples include: (a) You are at the shopping center with your friend. You see her take a pair of earrings from the rack and put them in her pocket. What do you do? (b) Your parents are gone for the evening. One of your friends comes over, and instead of getting a can of soda out of the refrigerator, he takes a beer. What do you do?

In addition to the cards, you need a tagboard "wheel" that lists a wide variety of options, such as (a) confront your friend and (b) do what they do to fit in. The wheel has a spinner attached. After the client has read the situation on a card picked from the stack, he or she spins the dial to the option that seems best and tells how they arrived at that decision.

Move it! A variation of the commercially produced game Twister (Milton-Bradley), this is popular with elementary students who need to work on social skills. You need a large plastic tablecloth. Use a magic marker to section off 12 squares, and color them different colors. Next, make a set of instruction cards with situations such as the following: (a) Your best friend makes fun of what you are wearing. What do you think, feel, and do? (Move on the board; right hand blue, left foot yellow); (b) The boy sitting behind you is spreading untrue rumors about you. What do you think, feel, and do? (Move; left hand green, right knee orange). This is a fun way to elicit discussion and problem solve about typical developmental situations. Cards can be tailored for a specific child.

Fish for feelings. This is a good game to use with 4-, 5-, and 6-year-olds to help develop awareness and expression of feelings. You need a set of tagboard fish labeled with feelings such as mad, sad, happy, scared, or worried. Each fish should have a hole in the nose. You also need a fishing pole (a short stick with a string attached to the end and a paper clip tied to the string). Lay the fish on the floor. As the child snags one, read the feeling word attached to the paper clip and ask the child to describe a situation in which he or she felt that way.

Circle of Self. Intended to help elementary aged clients develop a more global sense of self, this game utilizes a large tagboard circle with a spinner. The circle is divided like a pie into six dimensions: physical self, social self, emotional self, learning self, talent self, and things to improve self. The child spins the spinner, lands on a dimension, and describes him or herself according to that category.

Selected examples of commercially produced games include the following, available from Childswork/Childsplay:

Stop, Relax, and Think. This game, for children ages 6–12, is designed to teach impulsive children self-control. By moving a marker to four areas on the board, children learn to verbalize feelings, relax, and then problem solve to move ahead.

Coping and Decisions. This game is actually a series designed to increase awareness of positive and negative coping strategies, identify feelings in typical situations, and promote appropriate decision-making skills. This game is for use with 6- to 12-year-olds in individual or small-group counseling situations.

The Anger Control Game. This board game is recommended for 6- to 14-year olds who have anger- and temper-control problems. It can be used with 2–4 players. Areas emphasized in the game include distinguishing between aggressive and nonaggressive behavior and using self-talk to diffuse and control anger.

The Self-Concept Game. The purpose of this game is to teach children how to develop a more realistic attitude, minimize failure and negative reinforcement, and accept positive feedback. The game can be individualized for a client.

Communicate. As players compete for "good communicator" cards, they learn to enhance 29 social communication skills such as listening, asking for help, and making eye contact. It can be played with 2–6 players and is intended for use with 12- to 18-year-olds.

Literature

Bibliotherapy is the use of literature as a therapeutic counseling process. Gladding and Gladding (1991) identified two types of bibliotherapy: reactive and interactive. In the reactive format, the client is asked to read certain pieces of literature. It is assumed that, through character identification, the client can release emotions and gain new insights and ways to behave. The interactive model stresses guided discussion that occurs between the counselor and client concerning the literature, in an effort to help integrate the client's thoughts and feelings in response to the material.

Bibliotherapy has been used successfully for a wide variety of problems, such as divorce, promoting self-development, career awareness, and behavior change (Gladding & Gladding, 1991). It can be used in a classroom setting, as well as with small groups or individual clients. Literature selections can reflect typical developmental concerns and can be used with children who do not present major issues, or be applied more therapeutically with individuals who have varying degrees of emotional or behavioral problems.

For bibliotherapy to be effective, the counselor must have knowledge of appropriate literature. Materials cannot be too simple or too difficult. They should reflect the client's culture, gender, and age for identification to occur.

Fiction, nonfiction, poetry, self-help books, or autobiographies are examples of the types of literature used for bibliocounseling. For further information on appropriate selection of materials, consult Pardeck's (1984) *Young People with Problems: A Guide to Bibliotherapy* or the latest edition of *The Bookfinder* (Dreyer, no date), published by American Guidance Service. The *Bibliotherapy for Children and Teens Catalog*, published by Paperbacks for Educators, is also an excellent source for bibliotherapy materials.

Activity-Based Interventions

For lack of a better term, I have used *activity-based interventions* to describe a category of strategies that are designed to help children and adolescents deal with an aspect of a problem concretely. With this approach, the client performs an activity that provides insight or clarification, or is a behavioral intervention that teaches mastery. The following examples are a few of the activities that can be developed as part of the intervention process.

Interviews. The interview is a strategy that enables the child or adolescent to obtain information to expand his or her understanding of an issue. It can be used to help the client "normalize" the problem as well as be used rather paradoxically. For example, adolescents are prone to believe that their parents are the strictest, most old-fashioned, and stingiest of any they know. This viewpoint often creates a barrier between adolescents and their parents. By inviting the client to develop interview questions and "check out" other parents, he or she often comes to the realization that things are not as bad as they seem. The key is to work with the client to develop the questions in the session. Whether the adolescent actually does the interview is immaterial, the intervention has served its purpose by providing the youth with another perspective, as the following situation illustrates.

Fourteen-year-old Nicole was convinced that her parents were the worst of all. Having met with her parents on several occasions, the counselor did not find this to be the case. However, rather than jeopardize the relationship with Nicole by "taking sides," the counselor acknowledged Nicole's feelings and suggested that perhaps if she interviewed other parents she would have some concrete data to share with her folks in the hopes that they would change. Nicole did not think she should have to do any chores around the house or that she should have such an early curfew, among other things.

Nicole and the counselor developed several questions to ask her friends' parents: Does your son or daughter have to do any household chores? If so, what do they have to do? Do they get paid to do them? Are they grounded if they do not? Does your son or daughter have to be home at a certain time? What time? What happens if they are not? Nicole interviewed parents, but found to her amazement her situation was not all that bad.

Other ideas include having handicapped children interview others who have had to learn to cope with a disabling condition or interviewing parents about fears they had when they were young and what they did to overcome them.

Tape-recorded activities. This is an intervention best used with younger clients who still enjoy pretending. To help teach independent problem resolution, the counselor invites the child to first imagine that he or she is the child with the problem, and then to imagine being the counselor who is helping the child find a solution. This worked successfully with 6-year-old Leslie, who first pretended to be herself, explaining that she was worried about not doing well in school. She then switched roles and, as the counselor, asked if she was dumb, if she had not gotten stars in kindergarten, and if she could ask for help if she needed it. Although this is similar to role playing, the advantage is that the tape can be replayed and the learning can be discussed and reinforced more readily. Taping regular counseling sessions and giving the tape to the client to listen to during the week also is a good way to review concepts.

Using the media. Media can be incorporated readily into activity-based interventions. For example, middle school and high school clients can monitor television shows to look for such things as: (a) positive versus negative expressions of feelings, (b) consequences of decisions, (c) aggressive versus assertive behavior/communication styles, or (d) rational and irrational patterns of thinking and behaving. In this way, television can be used positively to expand a client's level of understanding, which in turn can be followed by the teaching of skills.

The newspaper can be used in a similar manner. Adolescents can be invited to cut out newspaper articles about problem events. They can bring the articles to the counseling session and engage in a rank-order activity, placing their particular problem in perspective along with the others. This helps those clients who seem to perseverate on the "awfulness" of their problems and do not seem to want to do anything to change.

Art Activities

Art activities usually are perceived by children as "nonthreatening and self-interpreted" (Riley, 1987, p. 21). They can engage clients in a process that helps them clarify and rectify problems. Art can be used in numerous ways as part of the counseling intervention process. Listed next are a selected few.

Masks. For young children who are afraid of the dark or monsters, having them make a mask to hang on the bedroom door or window has proved successful. As they create the mask, they can discuss their scary feelings with the counselor. Completing the activity can result in a feeling of power; they are in control of the situation.

Body outlines. The body outline can be used in a variety of ways: to facilitate self-awareness, to expand one's view of self to represent more global characteristics, or to help identify a variety of strengths and weaknesses to develop a realistic self-concept. The body outline is made by tracing the individual's body on paper. The way the outline is used depends on the purpose and the child's age level. For instance, the client can be invited to label and color in body parts or to draw arrows and identify strengths or weaknesses represented by various body parts.

Cartoons. Cartooning is used effectively to help identify possible solutions to conflict situations. Once the problem is identified, the young client can draw a cartoon strip or fill in ballooned parts of cartoon scenarios to illustrate various solutions. This technique also can be used as a means of catharsis and expression of feelings, where the cartoon figures simply represent the dilemma the child or adolescent is facing.

Graphics. Graphics—stick figures, lines, sketches, or marks—can be useful in the intervention process, both for the client and the counselor. For the client, graphics help them "see" the components or the factors that block their effective functioning. For the counselor, graphics offer another way to communicate with the client when words may be insufficient to explain a concept. Graphics can be used to illustrate complex relationships, generate alternatives, teach responsibility, and set goals (Nelson, 1987).

Music

"Music is more than just a medium of entertainment. It is a powerful tool that can capture attention, elicit long forgotten memories, communicate feelings, create and intensify moods, and bring people together" (Bowman, 1987, p. 284). Music is a form of communication that promotes positive mental health (Gladding, 1992). As Bowman reported, music can be used with children and adolescents to reduce anxiety, raise self-esteem, motivate slow learners, reduce disruptive behavior, and promote future planning. According to Gladding (1992), the effectiveness of this intervention depends on the client's involvement with music. In other words, if a youngster is passionate about music and readily identifies with a certain type or artist, the greater the likelihood that he or she will be assisted by this intervention. Two musical activities are described.

Self-composed music. Inviting young clients to compose lyrics/musical accompaniment to depict their own issue(s) is a powerful intervention. Through this medium they learn to express feelings, gain insight about problems, and identify ways to resolve dilemmas. Encouraging the child or adolescent to share his or her creation allows for a more direct discussion and clarification of issues.

Music/mood collages. Music is popular with children, and adolescents in particular. Because many of them listen to the radio or tapes for hours, they are very familiar with a variety of songs and learn to identify with specific songs in relation to a given mood or feeling. One activity that has proved helpful is to have clients make a tape of several of their favorite songs for a definite purpose: to relax, to feel happy, to be reflective, to be carefree, or to feel hopeful. They can play these taped selections when they want to experience that mood.

Drama

Gladding (1992) referred to the relationship between drama and life, noting that "healthy people . . . are able to change their behaviors in response to environmental demands. They are open and flexible and communicate in a congruent manner. Sometimes they become 'stuck' and 'dysfunctional' too, but in these cases they seek assistance" (p. 88). This author noted that, through drama, individuals can get "unstuck," gaining greater understanding of their roles and a clearer perspective.

Drama is especially appropriate for children and adolescents, who by their very nature love to pretend or be dramatic. As an intervention, drama allows young clients to assume different roles, try out new behaviors, clarify and express feelings, and problem solve.

Examples of dramatic activities to use with children and adolescents include the following.

Video drama. Although this cannot be done in an individual counseling setting, adolescents who have access to video cameras can be invited to make a video with a group of friends. A series of skits depicting ways to solve problems or a short play based on an issue relevant to their age group are examples of video productions. Gladding (1992) cited several advantages of video therapy: adolescents receive feedback about their behavior, they learn more about who they are through objective self-observations, they feel in control by operating equipment, and they are less resistant to adults because they focus on the equipment.

Role playing. Equally effective as an assessment strategy, role playing allows children to rehearse skills, learn new behaviors, view situations from multiple perspectives, gain confidence, and express feelings.

To structure the role play, the counselor can invite the client to play his or her own part and the counselor plays the part of the significant other person, or vice versa. It is best to use a very specific situation. Seventeen-year-old Robert used the role–play technique to practice telling his father that he had been fired from his job. Through the role play, Robert was able to learn a more effective way to share this information and anticipate possible reactions from his father.

A variation of the role play is the Gestalt Empty Chair technique (Gladding, 1992), which is excellent for dealing with guilt, indecision, anger, and other disturbing emotions. The client sits in one chair and has a dialogue with the empty chair about an issue (Gladding, 1992). When he or she feels like it, or as suggested by the counselor, the child shifts to the other chair and "talks back" to the first chair. A variation of this for younger children is to carry on a dialogue with a stuffed animal in the opposite chair.

Play

"The natural medium of communication for children is play and activity" (Landreth, 1987, p. 253). Through play, children are able to act out confusing or conflicting situations and learn to know and accept themselves. As noted by Ginott (1982), "the child's play is his talk and the toys are his words" (p. 145). For this reason, play is an exceptionally appropriate intervention for children, although the information they give us through play has to be interpreted in light of their current life situation and their developmental status (Garbarino & Stott, 1989).

Amster (1982) identified the following uses of play: (a) for diagnostic understanding, (b) to establish a relationship, (c) to facilitate verbalization, (d) to teach new ways of playing and behaving in daily life, and (e) to help a child act out unconscious issues and relieve tension.

Schaefer (1985) described three major approaches to play therapy, including psychoanalytic, structured, and the relationship approach. In the psychoanalytic approach, an interpretation of the child's actions and words provides the child with insight into unconscious conflicts. A wide variety of toys is available, and the child is free to select them. The structured approach is more controlled, with the counselor selecting the appropriate toys that facilitate working on an issue. The relationship approach is nondirective and stresses the importance of the counselor–child relationship. By creating an atmosphere in which the child feels accepted and understood, he or she can experience inner conflict and work toward resolution. A variety of materials is provided, and the child is free to select them.

Materials for play therapy should be selected to facilitate contact with the child, encourage catharsis and expression of feelings, aid in developing insight, and provide opportunities for reality testing (Ginott, 1982). Examples of materials include: (a) real-life toys, such as dolls, doll houses and furniture, play dishes, telephone, toy trucks, cars, and airplanes; (b) acting-out toys, such as dart guns, toy soldiers, rubber knives, Bobo clown, dart board, pounding bench; and (c) toys for creative expression, such as crayons, clay, paints, puppets, newsprint, and pipe cleaners (Landreth, 1987).

For a more thorough coverage of play therapy, the reader is encouraged to read *Play Therapy: Dynamics of the Process of Counseling with*

Children (Landreth, 1982) or *Handbook of Play Therapy* (Schaefer & O'Conner, 1983).

Puppets

Puppetry is a recommended technique with children and adolescents, because it provides a safe, comfortable way for children to share feelings, as well as a vehicle for learning alternative behaviors (Egge, Marks, & McEvers, 1987). James and Myer (1987) shared a variety of ways in which puppets have been used: (a) to establish trust and acquaint children to the counselor's role; (b) to teach positive attitudes about tasks; (c) to help children understand and express feelings about a traumatic event; (d) to act out relationship problems; and (e) to enhance their ability to express feelings, particularly anger and hostility.

Puppets can be selected to represent different personality types, such as the mischievous child, the perfect kid, the mean parent, the aggressive bully, or the fun-loving friend. Through identification with this fantasy-like person or animal, children begin to express themselves, and the counselor can help them learn to cope with their real-world problems.

SUMMARY

Without thorough problem assessment, appropriate interventions cannot be implemented. Likewise, without an intervention design process and knowledge about how to identify developmentally appropriate strategies, the counseling process is weakened. Understanding what needs to be done and how it can be accomplished are complex challenges that are simplified with an understanding of the developmental process and models that guide the design and implementation of intentional developmental interventions.

REFERENCES

Amster, F. (1982). Differential uses of play in treatment of young children. In G. L. Landreth (Ed.), *Play therapy: Dynamics of the process of counseling with children* (pp. 33–42). Springfield, IL: Charles C. Thomas.

Bauman, L. (1986). *The nine most troublesome teenage problems and how to solve them.* New York: Ballantine.

Bowman, R. P. (1987). Approaches for counseling children through music. *Elementary School Guidance and Counseling, 21,* 284–291.

Dreyer, S. (n.d.). *The bookfinder.* Circle Pines, MN: American Guidance Service.

Egge, D., Marks, L., & McEvers, D. (1987). Puppets and adolescents: A group guidance workshop approach. *Elementary School Guidance and Counseling, 21*, 183–196.

Garbarino, J., & Stott, F. (1989). *What children can tell us.* San Francisco, CA: Jossey-Bass.

Gibson, R. L., & Mitchell, M. H. (1990). *Introduction to counseling and guidance.* New York: Macmillan.

Ginott, H. (1982). A rationale for selecting toys in play therapy. In G. L. Landreth (Ed.), *Play therapy: Dynamics of the process of counseling with children* (pp. 145–152). Springfield, IL: Charles C. Thomas.

Gladding, S. T. (1987). Poetic expressions: A counseling art in elementary schools. *Elementary School Guidance and Counseling, 21*, 307–311.

Gladding, S. T. (1992). *Counseling as an art: The creative arts in counseling.* Alexandria, VA: American Association for Counseling and Development.

Gladding, S. T., & Gladding, C. T. (1991). The ABC's of bibliotherapy. *The School Counselor, 39*, 7–13.

Hutchins, D. E., & Cole, C. G. (1986). *Helping relationships and strategies.* Monterey, CA: Brooks/Cole.

James, R. K., & Myer, R. (1987). Puppets: The elementary school counselor's right or left arm. *Elementary School Guidance and Counseling, 21*, 292–299.

Landreth, G. L. (1982). *Play therapy: Dynamics of the process of counseling with children.* Springfield, IL: Charles C. Thomas.

Landreth, G. L. (1987). Play therapy: Facilitative use of child's play in elementary school counseling. *Elementary School Guidance and Counseling, 21*, 253–261.

Myrick, R. D. (1987). *Developmental guidance and counseling: A practical approach.* Minneapolis, MN: Educational Media.

Nelson, R. C. (1987). Graphics in counseling. *Elementary School Guidance and Counseling, 22*, 17–29.

Palmer, P. (1977). *The mouse, the monster, and me.* San Luis Obispo, CA: Impact.

Paperbacks for Educators. *Bibliotherapy for children and teens catalog.* Washington, MO: Author.

Pardeck, J. A. (1984). *Young people with problems: A guide to bibliotherapy.* Westport, CT: Greenwood Press.

Reynolds, S. (1993). Interventions for typical developmental problems. In A. Vernon (Ed.), *Counseling children and adolescents: A practitioner's guide* (pp. 55–84). Denver, CO: Love.

Riley, S. (1987). The advantages of art therapy in an outpatient clinic. *American Journal of Art Therapy, 26*, 21–29.

Schaefer, C. E. (1985). Play therapy. *Early Child Development and Care, 19*, 95–108.

Schaefer, C. E., & O'Conner, K. L. (1983). *Handbook of play therapy.* New York: Wiley.

Vernon, A. (1988). *Help yourself to a healthier you.* Minneapolis, MN: Burgess.

Vernon, A. (1989a). *Thinking, feeling, behaving: An emotional education curriculum for children.* Champaign, IL: Research Press.

Vernon, A. (1989b). *Thinking, feeling, behaving: An emotional education curriculum for adolescents.* Champaign, IL: Research Press.

Vernon, A. (1991). Nontraditional approaches to counseling. In D. Capuzzi & D. Gross (Eds.), *Introduction to counseling: Perspectives for the 1990s* (pp. 205–229). Denver, CO: Love.

Vernon, A. (1993). *Counseling children and adolescents.* New York: Love Publishing.

PART II

APPLICATION OF DEVELOPMENTAL THEORY: TYPICAL PROBLEMS, ASSESSMENT, AND INTERVENTION

Although dividing human development into age periods is somewhat arbitrary, it nevertheless is the most common way to look at what occurs at various stages of development. The following four chapters describe development across the life span of the school-aged child in these areas: self, social, physical, cognitive, emotional, and moral development. Each chapter outlines developmental characteristics of a specific period: early childhood (ages 4–5), middle childhood (ages 6–11), early adolescence (ages 12–14), and mid-adolescence (ages 15–18). Following these descriptions, five case studies illustrate problems typically experienced during this stage of development. The intent is to identify more of the "run of the mill" problems that helping professionals routinely encounter with children and adolescents. An overview of the problem, rather than a session-by-session account, is presented, along with a detailed description of developmental assessment and intervention strategies. Implicit in each example are the considerations for identifying appropriate assessment techniques and the four-stage intervention design process described in the first three chapters.

In addition to the case studies, other typical problems are identified for each developmental period to portray the range of concerns experienced by children and adolescents. Certainly what is presented has to be considered in light of several factors: the youngster's

69

environment, cultural values and expectations, socioeconomic status, parental support, coping responses, and prior success in mastering other developmental milestones. For some, typical concerns might be far more serious than those listed. For example, children who are sexually abused might not have the energy to worry about whether they are the last to be selected on a team. Teenagers living in alcoholic families might be more concerned about protecting their siblings from violent behavior during drinking episodes, than about whether they have to undress in front of peers in physical education class. On the other hand, many young people experience these typical concerns, in addition to the more serious problems within the family or the environment, making their maturation process even more complex.

Clearly, helping professionals must be prepared to assist young people with the spectrum of concerns they experience while growing up. In contemporary society, life is increasingly more complex and there are more challenges for children and adolescents: divorce; AIDS; physical, sexual, or emotional abuse; poverty; parental alcoholism; and homelessness. Unfortunately, many young people cope with these issues in self-defeating ways, through pregnancy, substance abuse, violence, or suicide, which in turn creates another layer of problems. Because these problems have become quite prevalent for a number of young people, I naturally have tended to overfocus on these major concerns and perhaps slight the normal, developmental concerns, which also need to be addressed for them to master developmental tasks successfully.

CHAPTER IV

EARLY CHILDHOOD:
ASSESSMENT AND INTERVENTION

Five-year-olds Eric and John were playing well together most of the afternoon, but Eric's mother could tell that things were beginning to deteriorate. She suggested that perhaps they needed to find a new activity. She volunteered to help them, stating that if they could each come up with several ideas, she would write them down and they could decide what to do. They each identified two or three things, and Eric's mother read the lists back, fully expecting that they would first choose an activity from one list and then try one from the other. Instead, they combined their ideas. John wanted to play "pets" and Eric mentioned "store," so they decided to play pet store, quickly transforming the playroom into a store for their stuffed animals.

It is amazing to see young children develop rudimentary problem-solving skills, use their imagination, and learn to get along with others. During these formative years, so many changes occur that affect later development. For some children, there are developmental delays; others progress normally. This chapter focuses on how to determine what is normal for the 4- and 5-year-old preschooler and how to design developmentally appropriate interventions for children who are experiencing varying degrees of difficulty with their growing up process.

CHARACTERISTICS OF YOUNG CHILDREN

Ironically, more instruction is available about how to balance a checkbook than about how to parent. Because of this lack of knowledge, parents rely on helping professionals for guidance about how their children are developing. In recent years, increased attention has been focused on early education and intervention with this age group. This is based on the recognition that, from a developmental perspective, the earlier the interventions are initiated, the more likely the success rate and the prevention of more serious difficulties (Hohenshil & Brown, 1991).

Following are descriptions of developmental characteristics for 4- and 5-year-old children in the areas of self-development, social development, cognitive development, physical development, emotional development, and moral development. This information provides the practitioner with a basis for assessing development and determining problems.

Self-Development

Sarafino and Armstrong (1986) described self-concept as "a detailed assessment of the whole person" (p. 413), stating that as children grow, their self-concepts become more detailed and complex. For instance, 4- and 5-year-olds have begun to define themselves. They know their name, can tell if they are a boy or girl, and whether they are big or little. Although they have a good idea of their competencies such as being able to count, tie a shoe, solve a puzzle, or have lots of friends, they do not have a global sense of their self-worth (Bee, 1992). At this age, children are very concrete and often focus on visible physical characteristics, such as what they look like, what they can do, or who they play with: "My name is Adam. I am five and I can ride a bike. I like to draw and play with my friend, Jake."

These children tend to be very egocentric, assuming that everyone thinks and feels as they do. They also believe that everything is alive, which is why they may believe that the Tooth Fairy took their tooth and left a quarter, or why a monster seems real. Preschoolers' self-esteem is generally quite high, and they tend to overestimate their abilities, thinking that they are competent in everything (Harter, 1983). They also have specific, stereotypical ideas about what is gender-appropriate.

Social Development

Play serves an important role for children, both in their own skill development and also in relation to others. Associative play characterizes 4-year-olds, where children interact and share, but do not actually seem to be playing the same game. At this age, children may talk about what they are doing and may be engaged in a similar activity, but there is not any common purpose. By age 5, they begin to be more cooperative: they take turns, create games, and elaborate on an activity. Usually, only one or two leaders organize activities, and children take on different roles within the group (Charlesworth, 1983).

With regard to friendship, Selman (1980) found that preschool children are most likely to be in Stage 0, momentary playmateship, or Stage 1, one-way assistance. In Stage 0, children are egocentric and cannot see another child's point of view. They have difficulty separating themselves to see a physical action and the intention behind it. If someone takes a toy, they cannot understand that the other child thought he or she had a right to take it. Friends are chosen based on a physical characteristic, such as "I like her because she has long hair," or because of what the friend has, such as a toy or candy.

At Stage 1, children do not understand give and take; they may see that a friend can help them, but do not necessarily see that they can help the friend. They are beginning to differentiate between their point of view and those of others. Friendships are characterized by one person taking the lead and another following, and the friendship ends if the follower does not follow.

Children at Stage 1 prefer same-gender playmates and show noticeable gender differences in play behavior. For example, boys take up more physical space in their play and are more interested in being rough and noisy: wrestling, running, pushing, or playing war. Girls are more inclined to engage in nurturant activities, such as playing house, cooking, playing with dolls, and helping each other. Girls' play is more cooperative, whereas boys' activities are more aggressive (Berger & Thompson, 1991; LeFrancois, 1992). Maccoby (1980) noted that these trends are true across cultures.

Cognitive Development

Preoperational thought patterns characterize the cognitive development of 4- and 5-year-olds (Bee, 1992; LeFrancois, 1992; Santrock & Yussen, 1992). Although they become increasingly more adept at relating symbols to each other in meaningful ways, they cannot relate them in a consistently logical way. Thus, they generally can reason logically in a familiar context about familiar things, but are not as logical if they have to reason about things they do not know about (Garbarino & Stott, 1989). For example, they can reason logically about their play activities, but have difficulty with something abstract such as death or divorce. Children of this age also have problems understanding the idea of reversibility. If they always walk to school and are asked for the first time to walk home, they probably will not understand the process of walking *to* school simply needs to be reversed.

Also characteristic of their cognitive style is what Piaget described as *centration* (Berger & Thompson, 1991). Centration refers to the tendency to center on their perceptions, rather than on a broader view of an experience or a situation. Berger and Thompson (1991) cited an example of centration: if the sun is shining through the bedroom window, it is time to get up even if it is 5:00 a.m. on Saturday morning. Because of this tendency to center on one idea, Flavell (1985) noted preschoolers understand things in terms of an either/or framework. For example, it is very difficult for a parent to explain to a child this age that he or she is not good or bad, but, rather, is a person who sometimes acts good and sometimes acts badly.

Centering on one aspect, rather than on the relationship of situations, also interferes with preschoolers' ability to understand cause and effect. For example, instead of realizing that they fell down because they were running too fast, they might blame someone else (Berger & Thompson, 1991). Centration also affects children's ability to take a perspective other than their own and their ability to see that the same object or situation can have two identities, one real and one apparent (Flavell, 1985). For instance, many preschoolers cannot understand that their mothers could also be a doctors; to them, you either are one or the other, but certainly not both simultaneously.

Language progresses rapidly during this period of growth. By age 5, children can understand almost anything explained to them in context and with specific examples (Berger & Thompson, 1991). Their vocabulary reflects their concrete stage of development. However, they have few abstract nouns such as *freedom*. They also have difficulty with concepts such as time and space, asking "are we there yet?" 5 minutes after the car has left the driveway for a 2-hour trip. Elkind (1991) cautioned that, although young children may be verbally precocious, they may not be as advanced cognitively. It is important to be aware that a discrepancy may exist. For example, although they can use the word <u>dead</u> accurately in a sentence, their understanding of death is that someone went away for awhile. It is not uncommon for a 5-year-old to ask when his dog is coming inside when he has just seen it buried.

Young children's ability to recall past events is more limited, and they are more likely to omit details (Garbarino & Stott, 1989). However, the more relevant the experience is to them, the more likely they are to recall it with greater accuracy. Concrete props can assist with memory recall, such as use of anatomically correct dolls with child sexual abuse victims. Garbarino and Stott (1989) also suggested asking specific questions such as "Did you play with blocks at school?" rather than simply asking what they did that day, which likely will be answered with "nothing" (p. 58).

Imaginative play and vivid fantasies characterize this period of development. Rubin, Fein, and Vandenberg (1983) noted the increased frequency and complexity of pretend play between the ages of 2 and 6. Although the 2-year-old may play with a cup and pretend to drink from it, the 4-year-old may also do this, but then will quickly transform the cup into another object, such as a rocket. By age 5, the pretend play objects can be entirely intangible, such as the existence of imaginary friends.

Physical Development

Significant physical changes occur in early childhood, but by the preschool years growth is slower. The child loses baby fat and becomes slimmer, and by age 6, body proportions are similar to those of an adult. Normal weight for a 6-year-old is 46 pounds and normal height is 46 inches (Berger & Thompson, 1991), but this varies depending on genetic background, nutrition, and health care. Boys tend to be more muscular and have less fat than girls. During the preschool years, it is not uncommon for children to have smaller appetites.

Although influenced by heredity and environment, age-related patterns of activity level are linked to brain maturation. It generally is acknowledged that activity level decreases each year after the first 2 years of life, but research suggests that it is a mistake to expect young children to be still for long periods of time. Because activity level also is associated with the ability to concentrate and think before acting, it is important to take this into account when structuring activities or behavioral expectations for the preschool child (Eaton & Yu, 1989).

Gross motor skills, such as running, jumping, throwing, and climbing, improve markedly during the preschool years, and 4- and 5-year-olds can climb ladders, play ball, and ride a tricycle. Fine motor skills that involve small body movement are more difficult to develop. For example, using a pencil, tying a bow, or pouring without spilling are challenges, because most children have not developed the necessary muscular control (Berger & Thompson, 1991).

Emotional Development

Because they lack an ability to verbalize their feelings, young children tend to express them directly through action (Elkind, 1991). The way emotional expression is modeled in the family directly influences children's reactions to feelings such as anger, fear, happiness, sadness, and affection. Thus, 4- and 5-year-olds are not able to understand that it is possible to have simultaneous emotions about a situation (Harter & Buddin, 1987), but they can understand the experience of different emotions at different times. Harter and Buddin cautioned that adults often want children to acknowledge mixed emotions, but this may be impossible. Rather, children should be encouraged to think about a time they felt positive about someone and a different time when they felt angry with this same person.

Moral Development

Preschool children are in what Kohlberg defined as the preconventional level of moral judgment (Berndt, 1992). In this stage, they assume that adults determine what is wrong and right. Their moral reasoning is dominated by concerns about the consequences of their behavior (Newman & Newman, 1991). Newman and Newman emphasized that children need to understand the consequences of their behavior on others to develop a basis for making moral judgments. Although many 4- and 5-year-olds struggle with this concept, it is nevertheless important to begin relating behaviors to moral principles (telling the truth, respecting others' feelings, and respecting authority) so that these are integrated into the children's concepts of right and wrong.

Several authors (Berndt, 1992; Newman & Newman, 1991; Turiel, 1983) cited an important distinction between moral rules and social conventions, emphasizing that social conventions differ across cultures. According to Newman and Newman (1991), a moral rule would involve stealing another child's toy, whereas a social convention would be whispering during sharing time or wandering away during large-group time. These authors indicated that 4- and 5-year-olds are able to understand that moral transgressions are wrong, because they affect others' welfare and are more consistent across settings, whereas social transgressions are disruptive and may depend on the situation. In other words, at home it might be permissible to get up from the table during dinner, but there is a rule against leaving the table during snack time at school.

Turiel (1983) proposed a third domain in addition to morality and social convention. He described the personal domain as one that does not involve the rights or welfare of others, nor directly affects the functioning of a system. For instance, if the parent of a 5-year-old says he or she cannot play with a friend, this child would not assume automatically that the parent was correct, as Kohlberg's stages of moral development indicated. Because the child distinguishes a personal issue from a moral rule, he or she does not automatically consider this a fair decision. This personal domain is important to know when assessing children's moral development.

The remainder of this chapter discusses special considerations in working with parents of 4- and 5-year-olds, followed by a variety of problems typically presented by preschool children or reported by parents and significant others. Examples of developmental assessment procedures are identified, followed by specific developmentally appropriate interventions.

PARENTAL INVOLVEMENT WITH YOUNG CHILDREN

When parents of young children bring them to counseling, they frequently feel inadequate and guilty: "We should have been able to prevent this problem from occurring. What's wrong with us?" They also may feel powerless: "Why does our child act this way? What can we do about it?" Parents may be particularly vulnerable as their children reach the preschool years. As children spend more time away from home, it becomes more difficult to control other environmental factors that may affect them. The helping professional may need to work directly with parents on some of these issues if their negative emotions interfere with their ability to implement appropriate interventions. Krista's situation illustrates this point.

According to her parents, 4-year-old Krista was the perfect only child until she started preschool the previous month. Since then, there had been dramatic behavior changes: temper tantrums or tears when it was time to leave for school, resistance about sleeping alone in her room, and refusal to leave the yard to play with friends. Although the counselor explained to the parents that these behaviors indicated some separation problems that were quite typical for 4-year-olds, the parents continued to feel responsible for Krista's misery, because they were forcing her to attend preschool. Because of this attitude, they were unable to implement any of the behavioral interventions the counselor suggested. The counselor realized that even if she worked directly with the child, the efforts would be sabotaged by the parents' beliefs about "poor little Krista."

These parents agreed to meet again with the counselor, who explained that their feelings stemmed from their beliefs that Krista should not experience discomfort, that they were responsible for the discomfort, and that it was easier to give in to Krista than to experience more conflict. By working through these beliefs, the parents gradually reduced their guilt feelings and employed effective behavioral interventions. Coupled with bibliotherapy and play therapy techniques that the counselor used with Krista, the problems disappeared in a short time.

Parents and helping professionals concerned about healthy development for young children have identified the following goals:

1. Helping develop a positive self-image.
2. Enhancing social and emotional development.
3. Encouraging independent thinking and developing problem-solving skills.
4. Improving communication skills.
5. Stimulating interest in the natural world.
6. Increasing capability for self-discipline.

7. Advancing the development of fundamental motor skills and abilities.
8. Identifying special individual mental, social, and physical needs.
9. Furthering the development of respect for human dignity and the rights of others.
10. Promoting aesthetic appreciation and expression.
11. Encouraging creativity.
12. Giving and receiving sincere affection. (Hohenshil & Brown, 1991, p. 8)

Despite the best efforts, many children "fall between the cracks" for one reason or another, and more directed attention is needed for them to achieve these goals.

Another factor to consider is the child's temperament. According to Chess and Thomas (1984), children are born with reliable and consistent patterns of behavior, such as activity level, regularity, adaptability, approach or withdrawal, physical sensitivity, intensity of reaction, distractibility, persistence, or positive or negative mood. These individual temperament differences explain why some children are more prone to act in certain ways and why they experience things differently. Their problems may have little bearing on what is developmentally typical. As an example, according to normal development, a child's activity level decreases with age (Eaton & Yu, 1989), but a child whose temperament is active may not experience this decrease to the same degree; that's just the way he or she is. That does not preclude the development of appropriate interventions, but it does shed a different light on the problem.

PROBLEM ASSESSMENT AND INTERVENTION: SELECTED CASE STUDIES

The problems selected represent a variety of what practitioners might expect from 4- and 5-year-olds. They range from typical developmental problems, which many children experience with varying degrees of difficulty, to more serious problems some children experience, because of family or environmental circumstances or a lack of ability to successfully master developmental tasks to achieve healthy development. With each example, a brief overview of the problem is outlined, followed by a sample assessment procedure and possible interventions. The intent is to illustrate a variety of problem assessment and intervention strategies appropriate for this age group, rather than to present detailed case histories with multiple, complex problems.

Problem One: Four-Year-Old Mark

Problem Overview

Mark's adjustment to preschool had gone smoothly, with the exception of swim class. His father informed the teacher that he had given up on lessons, because Mark was so terrified of the water, unlike his 8-year-old brother. According to the father, there seemed to be no reason for the fear. To his knowledge, Mark had never seen anyone drown or get hurt in the water, and he did not have other fears like this. The teacher indicated that the school counselor might be of assistance.

Developmental Considerations

Preschool children can reason logically about things they know about (Garbarino & Stott, 1989), but when experiencing an unfamiliar situation, it is not uncommon for children to exhibit some degree of anxiety. Due to their level of cognitive development, it is important to be as concrete as possible in the assessment and intervention process.

Assessment

Prior to meeting with Mark, the teacher mentioned that he was not a very verbal child and that he probably would be reluctant to talk. Therefore, the counselor filled a cake pan with water and some small plastic figures and set it on the table before Mark entered the office. The counselor indicated to Mark that lots of kids his age were afraid of the water, and that he would work with Mark on this problem. The counselor then pointed to the pan of water and the figures and asked Mark if he could show him what he was afraid of in the water. At first Mark just sat there, but finally he used one figure to push another into the water. As the counselor reflected on what had just occurred, he asked Mark if this had ever happened to him. Mark replied that his brother had tried to do it and had called him a baby because he was afraid. The counselor asked if anything else frightened him, and Mark shoved the figure down into the water and held him, indicating that he was drowning. When asked if there were other worries, Mark shook his head.

Intervention

The counselor selected *Wiggle-Butts and Up-Faces* (Kolbisen, 1989) to read to Mark. The main character, Alex, is a 4-year-old who learns to deal with his fear by teaching his stuffed animals how to breathe, float, and kick, and by practicing in the bathtub. After discussing the story, the counselor encouraged Mark to try these things at home. The next time they met was during the class swimming period. The counselor and Mark sat on the side and, as Mark observed, the counselor asked him some directed questions such as "Did you see anyone drown? Did you see anyone get pushed in? Did you see kids having fun? Did you see adults around to help kids if they got in trouble or were scared?" The next week he convinced Mark to put on his swimming suit and sit with him again to observe. The following week he encouraged Mark to sit on the edge of the pool. The counselor also gave him several self-statements to practice: (a) If something bad happens to me there are adults to help; (b) it looks like swimming can be fun and I might have fun, too; and (c) I've never seen anyone drown so it probably will not happen to me.

During the next several weeks, Mark gradually worked his way into the water, first for 3 minutes, then 5 minutes, then 10. He was encouraged to practice the self-statements each time before he went in the water and to practice at home with his stuffed animals.

Evaluation

The combination of bibliotherapy, self-statements, and behavior therapy ultimately was effective in helping this youngster overcome his fear of swimming.

Problem Two: Four-Year-Old Darrell

Problem Overview

Darrell is a middle child with four other siblings. His parents recently separated and Darrell, in particular, is having difficulty with this, because he is very close to his father who moved out and filed for divorce. Darrell cries a lot, both at home and at preschool. His appetite is poor and he has trouble getting to sleep at night. The relationship between the parents is not good, and Darrell sees his father infrequently.

Developmental Considerations

Because of their preoperational thought patterns, children at this age have difficulty understanding change and abstract concepts (Garbarino & Stott, 1989). They may personalize the situation due to their egocentric thinking (Scherman & Lepak, 1986), and assume they have done something wrong to make the parent leave (Neal, 1983). Boys may be more vulnerable to divorce than girls (Block, Block, & Gjerde, 1986). Despite that they are young, it is important to communicate with them truthfully, sensitively, and directly.

Assessment

The school counselor spoke with the mother who indicated these symptoms started when the family turmoil began. She seemed overwhelmed and uncertain about what to do with Darrell, indicating that her older boys appeared to be getting along all right and the babies were unaware of the circumstances. The counselor sensed that she would have to work individually with Darrell to help him deal with the situation as best as possible.

Working with Darrell, the counselor had him draw a picture of his family to get a sense of family dynamics and to help him begin to verbalize about the separation. Darrell drew his father in a separate house by himself and readily told the counselor that his dad did not live with them. When asked how he felt about it, he began to cry. The counselor needed to know what this child's perceptions of the situation were to help him more specifically. She set out some puppets, a toy phone, and a playhouse with family figures and used a structured play therapy approach to help Darrell depict the family conflict. It became apparent that, shortly before his dad left, Darrell had been a "bad boy" and blamed himself for the separation. Through his play, the counselor also noted that Darrell was afraid that his dad was mad at him and did not love him anymore, but still held out hope for him coming back home.

Intervention

To initiate more discussion about Darrell's feelings, the counselor made a feelings game, using a sheet of tagboard and constructing a dial that would spin and land on one of five paper plate faces expressing happy, sad, mad, worried, and scared. Each time his spinner landed on a face, Darrell was invited to talk about the feeling as it related to his present situation. He seemed most upset about why his dad had left home, repeatedly saying that it was his fault. This is particularly understandable for children this age if there has not been a lot of overt conflict or anything else immediately observable that would help explain the situation. The counselor helped Darrell clarify that he was not responsible by reading *Please Come Home: A Storybook About Divorce* (Sanford, 1985). She also adapted situation cards from the game *My Two Homes: A Game to Help Kids Understand and Accept Divorce* (Shapiro, 1992), designed to dispel common myths that confuse and upset children, which helped Darrell understand more about this situation. The counselor suggested that to help Darrell get to sleep at night, he sleep with his favorite stuffed animal or listen to *Imagine Yourself to Sleep,* a guided imagery tape. The counselor continued to meet twice a week with him, utilizing a combination of play therapy, drawing, and biblio-therapy to help him deal with his depressed feelings about the family situation.

Evaluation

Although the situation at home did not change, gradually Darrell began to feel better, crying less and eating and sleeping more normally, according to his mother. Because separation and divorce represent a significant disruption for young children, early intervention can help with later adjustment.

Problem Three: Five-Year-Old Adam

Problem Overview

Adam's teacher referred him to the school counselor. The teacher expressed concern that Adam, a normally outgoing and rather boister-ous boy, appeared very frightened about singing on stage with his class during the holiday program. Although he did not verbalize this to his teacher, she noticed that during rehearsal he was shaking and did not open his mouth. As soon as he got to the room, he ran to the bathroom. When she asked him what was wrong, he remained silent. Because the counselor was coming to their classroom later that day, the teacher explained the situation to him and asked if he could visit with Adam afterward. Adam is the youngest child and has three older sisters who are actively involved in music and dance activities.

Developmental Considerations

New experiences can be overwhelming for preschoolers, and it is not uncommon for them to be somewhat fearful. Their anxiety is height-ened, because they worry about being punished by the teacher (Youngs, 1985).

Assessment

Adam liked the counselor and willingly went with him, but, after receiving a negative response when asked if there was anything Adam would like to talk about, the counselor decided to indirectly assess the problem through a mutual storytelling technique (Gardner, 1971). Knowing that Adam liked animals and spent time with his father at the vet clinic, the counselor started the story with this sentence: "Once upon a time there was a little puppy who had to go to a strange place. Even though there were other animals there he still felt. . . ." At this point, the counselor turned the story over to Adam, who just sat and looked at him. The counselor probed a bit, asking how Adam thought the puppy might feel, and this time Adam said he probably was scared and mad, because he wanted to play instead of going there. The counselor asked what the puppy did when he was scared, and Adam said that he cried, but he did not let the other animals see him cry, because he did not want them to know that he was scared or they would make fun of him. The counselor asked him if the puppy ever got scared like that in other places, and he said no.

Based on these responses, the counselor could see that Adam probably was scared about performing and would have preferred to stay in the room and play. However, he did not want his classmates and possibly his sisters to know that he was scared enough to cry. Although this did not appear to be a case of generalized anxiety, it still was not clear why Adam was afraid. To find out more about this, the counselor encouraged Adam to continue his story about why the puppy would be scared. Adam replied that the puppy sometimes peed on the floor, and if the other animals saw it they would laugh.

At the conclusion of the story, the counselor felt he had a good perception of the problem, but checked with the teacher and Adam's mother to see if there were any problems with enuresis. His mother indicated that occasionally when Adam was excited he did have a problem, but was not aware of anyone making fun of him because of it. She thought he could be somewhat intimidated, because he had seen his sisters perform successfully.

Intervention

When the counselor met with Adam the next day, he reminded him of the story and asked if he ever felt like the puppy did. This time Adam admitted that he did, and, although he talked about the holiday program, he did not bring up his fear about wetting his pants or anything about his sisters. To help Adam work through the problem, the counselor brought out several puppets and invited Adam to play with them, suggesting that he could pretend that the puppets were going to be performing in a program. Adam hesitated a moment and then picked up a boy puppet and handed another puppet to the counselor. Because he did not seem to know what to do once he had the puppet on his hand, the counselor pretended that he was talking to Adam's puppet, and said, "I'm scared to go up on that stage." Adam's puppet nodded its head, but did not say anything. The counselor's puppet then said, "I'm afraid I'll forget the words to the songs or that I might get so scared I'll wet my pants." This time Adam's puppet said that he was afraid of that, too, and that his sisters might make fun of him, because they never forgot their words. As they continued with the puppet play, his other fears came out as well.

To reach some resolution, the counselor picked up a different puppet who said, "I used to be scared like you are, but now I do not get so scared, because I think about something that really makes me happy and that keeps me from being so scared." This puppet also suggested that it helped to put something in his pocket to hold onto when he got scared, and asked Adam's puppet if he thought those ideas might work. The counselor then suggested that he and Adam talk about what the puppet had said, and asked Adam to think of the happy thought and what he could put in his pocket. After he had identified these, the counselor read him *Harriet's Recital* (Carlson, 1982), a story about a preschooler who overcame her fears about a dance recital. In the following session, he and Adam listened to a tape with soothing music and identified several self-statements ("Even if I forget the words, maybe no one else will even know it"; "Other kids make mistakes too") that he could tape over the music to help him relax. As final interventions, the counselor suggested to the teacher that she make sure that Adam had gone to the bathroom prior to leaving for the performance, and indicated to the parents that it might be helpful for them to share their memories of being on stage for the first time and any fears they had.

Evaluation

Fear of wetting themselves is one of the major stressors for kindergarten children, according to Youngs (1985). By using the relaxation tape, normalizing the fear, and having Adam select something tangible and comforting to touch during the performance, his level of anxiety decreased somewhat. Because this appeared to be an isolated situation, the counselor did not feel that it would be effective to continue to work on this problem with a 5-year-old until the anxiety-provoking situation was once again more immediate.

Problem Four: Five-Year-Old Leia

Problem Overview

During the summer just before first grade, 2 months after the birth of her sister, Leia began to complain about stomachaches and headaches. Normally very cheerful and social, she was whiny, tearful, and did not want to play with her friends. Her parents were eager to address the problem before school started. Prior to the onset of these symptoms, they had been considering counseling, because their daughter did not have a particularly good year in kindergarten. Her teacher was overcritical and, although she was very bright, Leia was nervous about doing well in school and pleasing her teacher.

Developmental Considerations

Teacher disapproval is a major source of stress for 5-year-olds (Youngs, 1985). Because they center on their own perceptions and think in terms of absolutes (Flavell, 1985), it is not unusual for them to assume that if one teacher was unkind, they all would be. Because they conceptualize things in either/or terms, it may be difficult to deal with temporary displacement with the birth of a sibling.

Assessment

The counselor first decided to direct assessment toward the family unit, asking Leia to draw a picture of her whole family. In her drawing, baby Susan was as large as Leia, positioned between her two parents, with Leia standing behind her mother some distance away. This confirmed the counselor's hypothesis that she was feeling somewhat displaced after the birth of her sister. In describing her picture, Leia indicated that she felt left out and sometimes felt sick, because then her mommy would pay more attention to her than to her sister.

Second, with the counselor serving as secretary, she used a series of unfinished sentences, such as the following, to assess the school situation.

1. The best thing about kindergarten was _____.
2. The worst thing about kindergarten was _____.
3. My kindergarten teacher was _____.
4. When I did my work at school I _____.
5. When I was at school I worried that _____.
6. If I made I mistake I _____.
7. When I think about first grade I _____.

Based on Leia's responses to this assessment activity, it was apparent that she had a lot of anxiety about doing well and was a perfectionist. She verbalized that she sometimes got stomachaches when she thought about first grade, because she was afraid her teacher would not like her or would be mean like the kindergarten teacher.

Although the counselor now assumed that Leia's reluctance to play with friends had more to do with not wanting to be away from her mother, she again used several open-ended sentences.

1. I like to play with _____.

2. If someone asks me to play and I do not want to, it is because
   _____.

3. Something that scares me in my neighborhood is _____.
4. My favorite place to play in my neighborhood is _____.

Prior to designing interventions, the counselor met with the parents to share and verify impressions. They concurred that Leia was ordinarily quite social and that the withdrawal began after the baby was born. They also saw evidence of perfectionism at school and in her violin lessons, stating that Leia often was very demanding of herself. The targeted areas for intervention were: dealing with the addition of the baby, the perfectionism, and the anxiety about first grade.

Intervention

The counselor first read *Abigail Addington Brown Leaves Home* (Waters, 1979), a story about a young girl who runs away from home because her parents do not pay as much attention to her after her brother is born. The story brings out the irrational thoughts that the child has about her family: that they do not love her as much as they love her brother, that he always will get more attention than she will, and that her parents do not want her around anymore. The counselor and Leia discussed her similar feelings, and the counselor helped her prepare a list of her worries about her "place" in the family to discuss with her parents at the next session. At that meeting, Leia was reassured, as was Abigail Brown in the story, that she was not less important, and she and her parents made plans to spend special time together.

To deal with the school and perfectionism issues, the counselor first read *Oops!* (Vernon, 1989), a story about a first grader making a mistake. She and Leia talked about the fact that no one is perfect and that her stomachaches develop when she starts to think that she always has to do everything exactly right. Because Leia was very verbal, the counselor invited her to dictate into a tape recorder her own story about how it was natural to make mistakes and how that did not make her a dumb kid. Next, the counselor asked Leia to describe a time when she thought her teacher had been mean and they role played this scenario, followed by a role play of how other teachers might act in the same situation. Leia also was invited to talk to her friends about what their teachers had been like to help her develop the perspective that all teachers were not mean.

Evaluation

Due to the parental involvement, Leia quickly began to feel better about her place in the family. Her parents began paying more attention to her and the frequency of the headaches and stomachaches declined. She was more willing to spend time with friends. Because the anxiety about school was in the future, the counselor continued to work with her over the course of the summer. Although there was still anxiety when school started, Leia was able to go into the situation knowing that her teacher would not necessarily be like her previous one, and that she did not always have to be perfect. Over time, there was improvement on this dimension as well.

Problem Five: Five-Year-Old Margaret

Problem Overview

Margaret lives with her father, stepmother, and 2-year-old brother. She attends preschool three mornings a week and enjoys going. She is quite verbal and outgoing, relates appropriately with peers, and is doing well academically in this setting. According to her parents, she is usually a happy, carefree child.

Margaret's parents are concerned, because she recently has developed a terrible fear of the dark, but she cannot explain to her parents what specifically bothers her. This results in bedtime problems. Thus far, the parents have tried giving her a reward for going right to bed (which has not worked) and lying down with her until she goes to sleep. Although she will go to sleep if they are in the room, her parents do not want this to continue.

Developmental Considerations

Nighttime fears are a common problem for young children and can have a disruptive effect on the child and family (Merritt, 1991; Robinson, Robinson, & Whetsell, 1988). Imagination and vivid fantasies are very characteristic of this stage of development.

Assessment

The counselor first met with the parents to discuss the points raised with the critical questions to learn more about the frequency, intensity, and duration of the problem, and to get a general developmental history. Having determined that nothing seemed out of the ordinary, the counselor prepared to meet with Margaret. Because she is normally a self-assured, verbal child, the rapport-building process was accomplished readily by engaging her in a dialogue with puppets to learn more about her and her family. Once Margaret was comfortable and the purpose of the counseling interview had been explained in simple terms, the counselor was ready to assess the fear of the dark.

"Margaret, I'd like you to show or tell me more about what makes you afraid at night. If you like, you may use these dolls and this play furniture to show what happens when you go to bed and it is dark." As Margaret enacted the bedtime process, the counselor asked directed questions to clarify what occurs. As Margaret continued, it became apparent that she is convinced that there is something in her closet that will come and get her when the lights are out. Through acting out the incident, Margaret revealed that she is afraid to tell her parents about this, because they always tell her to be a "big girl," and she does not think that they will believe her if she lets them know her real fears. The counselor asked her to draw a picture of it, and she drew a large, scary monster. After checking for other fears or traumatic events, it appeared that the monster was the source of the terror, and intervention could be directed accordingly.

Intervention

The counselor explained to Margaret that many 5-year-olds are afraid of the dark and develop fears of animals or imaginary creatures (Merritt, 1991; Newman & Newman, 1991). The counselor emphasized to her parents that this is a common, but not necessarily short-lived problem, and commended them for taking it seriously, because it seemed very real to their daughter. The counselor thought that, by empowering Margaret, she could help her deal with the fear. She invited Margaret to buy a very scary mask to hang on the inside of her closet door to scare the monster from coming out, or make a mask. Next, she read *Ghost's Hour, Spook's Hour* (Bunting, 1987), which described the feelings of a young child who is afraid of the dark and overcomes the fear. Finally, she brainstormed with Margaret and her parents about what else Margaret could do. Margaret suggested moving her bed so that it did not face the closet; her parents suggested buying her a big flashlight to use if she senses that the monster is in the room; and the counselor introduced the idea of a "monster hunt" before bedtime, checking in the closet and using some "monster spray" (empty hair spray can) to get rid of it.

Evaluation

Both the assessment and interventions were concrete and appropriate for a 4-year-old, which increased the likelihood that they would be effective. At this age, action rather than logic is important (Berger & Thompson, 1991), so checking for the monster, instead of trying to reason with the child that there is no such thing as a monster, is the best approach. Having several different alternatives, as well as good parental involvement, also strengthened the intervention. Because this is a very typical developmental problem that was "nipped early in the bud," the problem was resolved within a few weeks.

OTHER TYPICAL DEVELOPMENTAL PROBLEMS

Young children take things quite literally, therefore it is not uncommon for them to become easily frightened due to their interpretation of an event. Elkind (1991) shared the example of the young child who was told that when he returned home after preschool he could see his new "half brother." Because he was frightened by the thought of seeing half of a brother, he refused to go home. I can recall my son suddenly refusing to walk to day care after preschool with the high school student who had accompanied him every day for 3 weeks. When asked why he was frightened, he explained a police officer visiting school the previous day warned them not to go with strangers. In Eric's words, "I really don't know AnnaBeth too well; she's still a stranger."

Four- and 5-year-olds face uncertainty as they begin to experience new situations. They may be hesitant to leave the house to play in the yard, to visit a friend, or to be left at preschool, because they are afraid of separation from a parent. They also have numerous other fears, such as dark rooms, noise at night, large or wild animals, snakes, bodily injury, and bad people (Robinson, Rotter, Fey, & Robinson, 1991).

SUMMARY

All too often, parents and professionals have to be reminded that childhood is not an easy time, and that although a young child's problems may seem minor in comparison to those adults face, they are extremely significant to 4- or 5-year-olds who do not have the repertoire of coping mechanisms nor the verbal or cognitive skills to "put it altogether" and make sense of what they are experiencing. For this reason, the developmental assessment and intervention process are critical.

The goal of developmental assessment is to look at where children are relative to what is normal for a particular stage of development. In many cases, the problems are indicative of normal developmental issues, as illustrated by Adam's anxiety about wetting his pants, Margaret's fear of the dark, Leia's jealousy over a new sibling and anxiety about first grade, and Mark's swimming terror. The goal of the assessment then becomes twofold: to determine the severity of the symptoms (do they go beyond what would be considered typical for a problem of this nature?) and to design assessment procedures appropriate for the child at this age. If the problem is something many children commonly experience, but not reflective of a normal developmental issue, as in the case of Darrell, the goal of the assessment is to determine if the child's conceptualization of the problem and response to it corresponds to what is characteristic of this developmental period or if the child has regressed significantly.

Fortunately, with the increased awareness regarding the importance of prevention and early intervention with young children, many strategies may be employed with these clients.

Examples of age-appropriate interventions described in this chapter included bibliotherapy, visual arts, behavioral techniques, therapeutic games, and role play. By utilizing a wide variety of developmentally based interventions, parents and professionals can collaborate on the most effective way to address problems.

REFERENCES

Bee, H. (1992). *The developing child.* New York: HarperCollins.

Berger, K., & Thompson, R. (1991). *The developing person through childhood and adolescence.* New York: Worth.

Berndt, T. (1992). *Child development.* Orlando, FL: Harcourt Brace Jovanovich.

Block, J. H., Block, J., & Gjerde, P. (1986). The personality of children prior to divorce: A prospective study. *Child Development, 57,* 827–840.

Bunting, E. (1987). *Ghost's hour, Spook's hour.* New York: Clarion.

Carlson, N. (1982). *Harriet's recital.* Bergenfield, NJ: Penguin.

Charlesworth, R. (1983). *Understanding child development.* Albany, NY: Delmar.

Chess, S., & Thomas, A. (1984). *Origins and evolution of behavior disorders: From infancy to early adult life.* New York: Brunner/Mazel.

Eaton, W. O., & Yu, A. P. (1989). Are sex differences in child motor activity level a function of sex differences in maturational status? *Child Development, 60,* 1005–1011.

Elkind, D. (1991). Development in early childhood. *Elementary School Guidance and Counseling, 26,* 12–21.

Flavell, J. H. (1985). *Cognitive development* (2nd ed.). Englewood Cliffs, NJ: Prentice-Hall.

Garbarino, J., & Stott, F. (1989). *What children can tell us.* San Francisco, CA: Jossey-Bass.

Gardner, R. (1971). *Therapeutic communication with children: The mutual storytelling technique in child psychotherapy.* New York: Aronson.

Harter, S. (1983). Developmental perspectives on the self-system. In P. H. Mussen (Series Ed.) & E. M. Heatherington (Vol. Ed.), *Handbook of child psychology, Vol. 4: Socialization, personality, and social development* (pp. 275–385). New York: Wiley.

Harter, S., & Buddin, B. J. (1987). Children's understanding of the simultaneity of two emotions: A five-stage developmental acquisition sequence. *Developmental Psychology, 23*, 388–399.

Hohenshil, T. H., & Brown, M. B. (1991). Public school counseling services for prekindergarten children. *Elementary School Guidance and Counseling, 26*, 4–11.

Imagine yourself to sleep. (1988). King of Prussia, PA: Childswork/Childsplay.

Kolbisen, I. M. (1989). *Wiggle-butts and up-faces.* Half Moon Bay, CA: I Think I Can.

LeFrancois, G. R. (1992). *Of children: An introduction to child development.* Belmont, CA: Wadsworth.

Maccoby, E. E. (1980). *Social development: Psychological growth and the parent-child relationship.* New York: Harcourt Brace Jovanovich.

Merritt, J. (1991). Reducing a child's nighttime fears. *Elementary School Guidance and Counseling, 25*, 291–295.

Neal, J. H. (1983). Children's understanding of their parents' divorces. In L. A. Kurdek (Ed.), *Children and divorce* (pp. 185–220). San Francisco, CA: Jossey-Bass.

Newman, B. M., & Newman, P. R. (1991). *Development through life: A psychosocial approach.* Pacific Grove, CA: Brooks/Cole.

Robinson, E. H., Robinson, S. L., & Whetsell, M. V. (1988). A study of children's fears. *The Journal of Humanistic Education and Development, 27*, 84–95.

Robinson, E. H., Rotter, J. C., Fey, M. A., & Robinson, S. L. (1991). Children's fears: Toward a preventive model. *The School Counselor, 38*, 187–192.

Rubin, K. H., Fein, G. G., & Vandenberg, B. (1983). Play. In P. H. Mussen (Series Ed.) & E. M. Heatherington (Vol. Ed.), *Handbook of child psychology: Vol. 4: Socialization, personality and social development* (pp. 175–235). New York: Wiley.

Sanford, D. (1985). *Please come home: A storybook about divorce.* Portland, OR: Multnomah Press.

Santrock, J., & Yussen, S. (1992). *Child development: An introduction.* Dubuque, IA: William C. Brown.

Sarafino, E. P., & Armstrong, J. W. (1986). *Child and adolescent development.* St. Paul, MN: West.

Scherman, A., & Lepak, L. (1986). Children's perceptions of the divorce process. *Elementary School Guidance and Counseling, 21*, 29–36.

Selman, R. (1980). *The growth of interpersonal understanding: Developmental and clinical analyses.* New York: Academic Press.

Shapiro, L. (1992). *My two homes: A game to help kids understand and accept divorce.* King of Prussia, PA: Childswork/Childsplay.

Turiel, E. (1983). *The development of social knowledge.* Cambridge, England: Cambridge University Press.

Vernon, A. (1989). *Thinking, feeling, behaving: An emotional education curriculum for children.* Champaign, IL: Research Press.

Waters, V. (1979). *Color us rational.* New York: Institute for Rational Living.

Youngs, B. B. (1985). *Stress in children.* New York: Arbor House.

CHAPTER V

MIDDLE CHILDHOOD: ASSESSMENT AND INTERVENTION

Many people have vivid memories, both positive and negative, about what it was like to be an elementary school student: sharing secrets with a "best friend," being picked last for a team, being selected as the teacher's "helper," or being teased by classmates. People may recall not being able to read or do math as well as some of their classmates, or being commended for outstanding verbal abilities. Throughout the grade-school journey, people continued to master various developmental tasks, some of which were more challenging and required more effort than others. Although many readily mastered these tasks, others struggled or suffered developmental delays in some areas.

Berger and Thompson (1991) contended these are the best years of the life span. According to these authors, it is easy to master new tasks, because physical development is almost "problem-free" (p. 331), and most children are able to learn quickly, think logically, and differentiate between right and wrong. They described this period as one in which children see their parents as helpful, their teachers as fair, and their futures as promising. They noted two clouds on the horizon, however: school failure and peer rejection.

Others have a different view of these early school years, citing increasing evidence of childhood stress (Youngs, 1985), the pressure to grow up "too fast, too soon" (Elkind, 1988), and the high percentage of children who suffer from emotional or other problems and need mental health services (Thompson & Rudolph, 1992). Despite that this is a more stable growth period than those preceding or following it (Berger & Thompson, 1991), helping professionals who routinely work with middle-aged children (ages 6–11) are aware that some children breeze through this period of development, whereas others get hung up due to a combination of personal and environmental factors. Although limited somewhat by their ability to conceptualize and verbalize what they are experiencing, this age group of children nevertheless needs support as they forge new territory.

In this chapter, descriptions of developmental characteristics are identified for the middle-aged child, ages 6–11. This information is followed by several examples of problems this age group experiences, accompanied by specific developmental assessment strategies and interventions.

CHARACTERISTICS OF MIDDLE-AGED CHILDREN

Although some contend that there are few meaningful changes during middle childhood, Collins (1984) viewed this period as part of a continuous process of development as well as a distinct phase with specific age-related changes. Perhaps most significant is the shift in cognitive processing between the ages of 5 and 7, which has important implications for other areas of development. There is growing evidence that behavior and performance during middle childhood have long-term implications for social and personal development in adolescence and young adulthood (Hartup, 1984).

As described in the following paragraphs, there are transitions and consolidations that occur during this period and contribute to the growth of children aged 6–12.

Self-Development

As their cognitive abilities mature, children's self-understanding expands and reflects others' perceptions (Collins, 1984). Their internal locus of control and assertiveness characteristic of independent behavior are beginning to evolve (Fadely & Hosler, 1980). They progress from explaining their actions by referring to events in the immediate situation (I hit her because she hit me) to relating actions to personality traits or feelings (I was upset about something else and just hit her). As their concepts of self become more integrated, they describe themselves in terms of several competencies at once: "I am tall, athletic, and smart in science." They also are more aware of characteristics such as values, goals, and ideals (Collins, 1984).

Marcus and Nurius (1984) outlined four critical self-concept tasks of middle childhood: developing a relatively stable and comprehensive self-understanding, clarifying an understanding of how the social world works, developing standards and expectations for one's own behavior, and developing strategies to control one's behavior. These authors contended that, in addition to understanding what is "me" and "not me" (p. 151), they begin to incorporate their behavioral standards into their self-concept, which becomes a basis for self-evaluation.

Other factors also contribute to self-evaluation. As they begin to compare their skills and achievements to others, they become self-critical, feel inferior, or may experience a decrease in self-esteem (Ruble, Boggiano, Feldman, & Loebl, 1980). Although especially true for girls, children during this period tend to blame themselves (rather than bad luck) for their deficiencies (Stipek, 1984). As they more readily differentiate the areas in which they are more or less successful, they start to take failure more seriously, which in turn negatively impacts self-esteem. Harter (1983) posited that self-esteem reaches a low at age 12 before it starts to rise gradually in the teenage years.

During this period, children are vulnerable to "learned helplessness"; they are more inhibited about trying new things, because they are aware that they have failed in the past and may be unable to do anything to improve their performance (Dweck & Elliott, 1983).

A factor influencing self-development in these school-aged years is peer influence. As children strive to achieve new skills, they are subject not only to their own self-evaluation, but to feedback from peers as well (Harter, 1982). They become aware of their specific areas of competence, and may approach the process of self-evaluation with either self-confidence or self-doubt, depending on how they resolved tasks in early years (Newman & Newman, 1991).

Social Development

Socialization in the context of a peer group becomes a central issue for the middle-aged child. Acceptance in a group and a "best friend" contribute significantly to a child's sense of competence (Berger & Thompson, 1991). Dealing with peer group pressure, rejection, peer approval, conformity, and intimate friendships are salient issues. Throughout this period, their friendships become increasingly more intense and intimate, particularly for girls, and they choose best friends who are of the same gender and race, tending to be antagonistic toward the opposite gender (Berndt, 1981; Hartup, 1983). As they grow older, their friendship patterns become more rigid, making it difficult for an outsider to join an established group. The size of their friendship network also decreases with age, although boys tend to have larger and less intimate networks (Berger & Thompson, 1991). Although parents remain an important source of support, children at this age are becoming more dependent on friends for help in academic and social situations, and by age 10 or 11 may not want to be kissed by parents in public (Berger & Thompson, 1991).

Although physical aggression and quarreling decrease during this period, there are more abusive verbal exchanges, such as insults and derogatory comments. Competition also increases with age, although this varies somewhat according to culture (Hartup, 1984).

Social skills, cooperative behavior, and self-esteem can be developed through participation in clubs such as scouts and 4-H. Team play is a new dimension of social development, which helps children learn to give and receive feedback, to value their role as part of a larger system, to experience personal satisfaction from victories and frustration from defeat, and to contribute to team goals (Newman & Newman, 1991).

By age 7, children begin to outgrow their egocentrism and develop more prosocial behaviors, such as sharing a lunch or showing concern for others (Berger & Thompson, 1991). They also can perform role-taking operations (Cooney & Selman, 1980; Selman, 1971). This implies that children are developing the ability to view the world as well as self from another's perspective, and can begin to infer another's capabilities, attributes, feelings, expectations, and potential reactions. They are better able to interpret social cues (facial expressions, vocal intonation) and communicate information to listeners (Hartup, 1984). Selman (1971) saw these as important social skills, noting that taking another's perspective includes being able to differentiate the other's point of view from one's own and acquiring the ability to shift, balance, and evaluate input. As a result, middle-aged children are much more adept at social problem solving and can master a variety of alternatives for resolving conflict.

During this period, children are intent on belonging and developing a social identity in relation to familiar roles, such as friend, student, scout, or team member (Hartup, 1984).

Cognitive Development

During this school-aged period, vast differences occur in cognitive development. According to Piaget (1967), a transitional period between preoperational and concrete operational thought occurs between the ages of 5 and 7, but by age 7 or 8, children are definitely concrete operational thinkers. As such, middle-aged children are able to understand logical operations, such as identity (the content of an object remains the same even if the appearance changes), reversibility (a process can be reversed into the original form), reciprocity (a change in one dimension effects a change in another), and classification (categorizing objects by classes). These principles can be applied in many contexts, such as friendships, rules in games, or team play.

School-aged children's thinking is characterized by a broader grasp of underlying assumptions, rational thought, and more comprehensive logic (Santrock & Yussen, 1992). They acquire new ways to organize facts, and learn best by questioning, exploring, and doing (Flavell,

1985). Their problem-solving abilities are enhanced, and, as a result, they begin to view social and personal situations with more confidence.

Although language development is more subtle, children continually understand more about how language can be used, which results in more control of comprehension and use of language. They are able to understand more abstract concepts and can tailor vocabulary, sentence length, content, and nonverbal cues to the situation (Berger & Thompson, 1991).

Newman and Newman (1991) maintained that the most impressive area of growth during these middle years is in the acquisition of skills, particularly reading. They emphasized that the energy that middle-school-aged children apply to learning new skills is similar to that of a toddler who strives for competence and mastery.

Physical Development

This is a period of relatively stable growth for most children, although they grow taller, their body proportions change, and their muscles become stronger. According to Lowrey (1986), the average 10-year-old weighs about 70 pounds and is about 54 inches in height.

Maturation varies from child to child, and it is normal to find various rates of development, with some children undergoing puberty by age 10 or 11. This variation sometimes can be a source of distress for children who think they "look different" or who are noticeably lacking in physical skills as they compare themselves with others (Harter, 1983).

Due to the slow growth rate during this period of development, children have a high degree of self-control over their bodies and are not as clumsy as they become when they enter puberty, for example. They can master almost any motor skill, although some motor skills rely on reaction time, which is related to brain maturation. At this age, boys and girls are about equal in physical abilities, except that girls have better overall flexibility and boys have better forearm strength (Berger & Thompson, 1991).

Emotional Development

School-aged children's understanding of emotions positively impacts social relationships and self-perception. They are able to understand that a person can have two conflicting emotions simultaneously (happy that she got a new shirt, but sad because it was red instead of blue) and can rely more on inner experiences for clues about how others are feeling (Fischer & Bullock, 1984). These children have learned that feelings can change and that they are not the cause of another person's emotional discomfort (Carroll & Steward, 1984). Generally, children at this age are more sensitive and empathic and are becoming more able to communicate their feelings.

Moral Development

Most children under age 9 reason at Stage 1 of the preconventional level of moral judgment, reflecting the lowest level of development, because they do not consider social norms when making a decision. These children assume that adults define what is right and wrong. Gradually they move into Stage 2, where they look at more than one perspective and recognize conflict between perspectives (Berndt, 1992). However, because they only consider two perspectives, they contend that people should do what they want to or make a deal if there is conflict between them. The basis of their moral judgment is still individualistic, and they base their decisions on what meets their own needs and desires (Berndt, 1992). Peer interaction, which facilitates opportunities to take another perspective and generate new rules and standards, promotes moral development at this age, as do parent–child interactions and discussions about value-laden topics, according to Walker and Taylor (1991).

Colangelo and Dettmann (1985) found that children in Grades 3–5 were most concerned about moral issues relating to peer and family relationship issues; conflicts regarding honesty, cheating, stealing, and lying; and decisions about whether to intervene or report. Boys at this age also reported dilemmas about alcohol and tobacco. These practical, everyday experiences become sources of conflict for children as they strive to develop these moral skills.

PARENTAL INVOLVEMENT WITH MIDDLE-AGED CHILDREN

As children grow up and begin to experience new things, so do their parents. I vividly remember "our" first experience with grades in elementary school. When my son brought home a spelling test with a less-than-average grade, I immediately assumed he would be a poor speller forever and wondered what I should have done as a parent to prevent this from occurring. Luckily my 8-year-old was more rational than I was, putting it in perspective by saying, "Just because I got one bad grade doesn't mean that I'll flunk spelling. I just have to work harder." It became obvious to me that, although the teacher helped my child deal with the ramifications of this new set of circumstances, no one prepared me for this.

During this period of development when peers gradually become more important and families less, significant changes begin to occur in the way parents and children interact. Parent–child communication becomes increasingly important. Helping children learn to accept responsibility, deal with success and failure, and develop social skills are critical tasks.

Fortunately, the role of the counselor as consultant has expanded to provide parents with information about normal development and what to do when their children deviate from the norm (Dustin & Ehly, 1992; Hawes, 1989; Mathias, 1992). Parent education and support groups exist in many schools and communities to help parents deal with developmental issues and parenting skills; and with the special needs of the single parent, stepparent, parents with terminally ill children, or parents of mentally or physically disabled children, for example.

Although some may consider this middle childhood period one of relative stability (Berger & Thompson, 1991; Collins, 1984), children gain access to new settings and circumstances, which present them with developmental challenges. The role of parents, although somewhat diminished because teachers, coaches, peers, and other adults also exercise varying degrees of influence, is still critical.

PROBLEM ASSESSMENT AND INTERVENTION: SELECTED CASE STUDIES

It is interesting to speculate why some children negotiate developmental milestones with seemingly little difficulty, whereas others struggle with them. Even more perplexing is how some children experience incredibly negative circumstances and still achieve healthy development. Because middle childhood spans a number of years, children live through numerous "firsts," some stressful and some exhilarating, as their horizons broaden.

In this chapter, problems experienced by 6- to 11-year-olds are described. Problems selected represent both typical developmental issues as well as problems resulting from family circumstances. The intent is to provide the reader with examples of assessment and intervention strategies, rather than detailed case histories and complex problems.

Problem One: Six-Year-Old Stevie

Problem Overview

Stevie and his father had lived with Stevie's grandmother for the past 5 years. Last month, after a brief illness, she died. Since then, Stevie has said very little about the incident, but the school recommended counseling, because they noticed some regressed behaviors such as thumb sucking and enuresis. According to the father, Stevie and his grandmother were very close, and, since his mother left them when Stevie was a baby, the grandmother had been like a mother to him. Prior to the illness and death, Stevie was a well adjusted little boy.

Developmental Considerations

It is very painful, but yet common, for a young child to experience the death of a grandparent. The degree of attachment to the deceased is an important factor in the way the child experiences grief. Typically children aged 3–9 may experience adjustment disorders, psychosomatic disorders, depression, regression, or disruption of habits (Cunningham & Hare, 1989; Rando, 1984). Due to their level of cognitive development, children at this age have difficulty understanding an abstract concept such as death (Furman, 1984).

Assessment

Given that Stevie was very shy, the counselor decided to use play media to assess how he was feeling and what he was thinking. Before he entered the room, the counselor placed a basket of puppets and toys beside a small chair. After introducing himself to Stevie, the counselor informed Stevie that he knew something sad recently had happened when his grandmother had died, and that he would like to help Stevie talk about his feelings. He invited Stevie to play with the puppets or toys in the basket.

During the first session, Stevie held one of the stuffed animals, but did not talk. In the next two sessions, he used puppets actively to act out what it was like when his grandmother died. From this, the counselor learned that Stevie thought it was his fault that she died, because he had had a cold and his dad had said not to get too close to her so she would not catch it. Stevie also was afraid that he or his dad might die. He was afraid to go to sleep at night, because someone had told him that his grandmother was just sleeping, but then she never woke up again.

As a 6-year-old, it is likely that Stevie still has many preoperational thought processes that would explain why he personally feels responsible for his grandmother's illness (egocentric thinking) and why he is generalizing about this situation to his own life. Although these are fairly typical concerns for a 6-year-old, intervention is essential to help him deal effectively with this loss to stop the progression of the regressed behaviors.

Intervention

Play therapy in the form of sand play was used to help Stevie work through the sadness and guilt. Using a sand tray and a collection of figurines, Stevie was invited to create sand pictures. His first picture depicted his grandmother sick in bed, with his father scolding him to stay away. His next picture showed his grandmother in a box beside a big hole. His third picture showed him standing all alone, with his father off in the distance. As he created his pictures, he began talking more about his grandma's death and how he missed her. The counselor pointed out that he looked like he was all alone, and he began a dialogue with the father figurine, telling him how he did not mean to make his grandmother sick. In subsequent sessions, Stevie worked through his guilt and sadness using sand play.

Bibliotherapy also was used with this young client. Through reading *Grandpa's Slide Show* (Gould, 1987) and *Nana Upstairs, Nana Downstairs* (DePaola, 1973) to Stevie, he and the counselor were able to discuss how these stories related to his situation, clarifying misconceptions and helping him deal with his feelings through catharsis.

Evaluation

Parents of young children need to understand how their children are experiencing death and how to talk to them about what has occurred. In Stevie's case, after several sessions of play therapy and bibliotherapy, the thumb sucking and enuretic behaviors slowly began to decrease.

Problem Two: Seven-Year-Old Annie

Problem Overview

Annie's mother insisted that the "terrible 2s" had not been as bad as what she was experiencing with this second grader. On a daily basis, Annie blatantly refused to do what was asked of her, dominated all interactions with adults and other children, threw temper tantrums when she did not get her way, and, in general, was very unpleasant to be around. At school things were not quite as bad, but there was still a lot of domineering behavior and inappropriate aggression. Annie's sister is in fourth grade. Her father is a truck driver and is gone for part of the week, which leaves the mother in charge most of the time.

Developmental Considerations

Seven-year-olds want their parents' attention and can be self-willed. Although 7 is generally a calmer age than 6, children at this age tend to procrastinate and get distracted; when parents ask them to do something, it is not uncommon for them to resist, at least initially (Ames & Haber, 1985).

Assessment

The parents were first interviewed. After determining that this behavioral pattern had begun during the past year, with no parental knowledge of any precipitating event and no evidence of Attention Deficit Hyperactivity Disorder (ADHD) according to the evaluation conducted the previous year, the counselor asked what had been done to try to alleviate the behavior. For the most part, the parents sent Annie to her room when she misbehaved. But if this also happened in public, they either left the scene or continually reminded her to behave. Nothing they had done seemed to do any good, and they felt as if they were living with a walking time bomb. Although Annie spent more time with her mother, her behavior was consistent with both parents, as were their responses to her.

After hearing Annie's behavior described and discussing the frequency of these incidents, the counselor thought this sounded like a child who was attempting to assert herself, but had not developed an understanding of others' needs. The counselor asked the parents and teacher to complete a short locus of control checklist, developed by Fadely and Hosler (1980). The following questions (rated on a 1–10 scale) are included on this checklist, which is designed to determine how well a child is accepting personal responsibility and how adequately he or she has developed an internal locus of self-control:

1. Child asserts self in situations where peers attempt to dominate him or her?
2. Child displays appropriate assertiveness and competitive spirit?
3. Accepts adult supervision and limit setting?
4. Displays remorse in situations where he or she is reprimanded?
5. Recognizes his or her role in situations involving conflict?
6. Shows willingness to abide by rules of behavior and tends to judge others who misbehave?

This checklist includes 20 questions. In a reworded format, similar questions were asked of Annie: "Do you feel bad when your parents get upset with you? If your parents or teacher tell you not to do something, do you do as they ask?" Rather than mark a 1–10, Annie moved along a continuum of masking tape on the floor.

In analyzing the responses, it was apparent that Annie did not accept personal responsibility well and displayed an immature internal locus of control. Although these are problems children face as they begin to become independent, it became obvious that Annie was having difficulty and that intervention was necessary.

Intervention

To address this problem, the counselor decided to work with Annie and her parents. With Annie, she targeted the area of personal responsibility that entails learning to accept the consequences of one's behavior. She used two activities, *I Have To Have My Way* (Vernon, 1989), which illustrates the negative effects of demanding through a story and discussion questions; and an adaptation of *What Happens When* (Vernon, 1989), a series of role plays designed to help illustrate behaviors and consequences and who is in control. She also read *Instant Replay* (Bedford, 1974) to Annie to help her see that she could learn to change her behavior by pretending to do an "instant replay" of the situation to view it differently. The counselor and Annie practiced the concepts presented in the story by role playing relevant "instant replay" situations.

With Annie's parents, the counselor explained principles of natural and logical consequences (Dreikurs & Grey, 1970), indicating that it was important to help Annie evaluate her own behavior and make choices about the consequences. She had them share examples of problematic behaviors, and discussed how to apply logical consequences to a variety of situations.

Evaluation

Trying to change behavior is usually a long-term endeavor, as it was in this case. As the parents continued to learn more about logical consequences and apply them, the counselor worked with Annie, both individually and in a small-group setting, to develop a greater awareness of her behavior, to learn alternatives to aggressive behavior, and to interact cooperatively with peers and adults.

Problem Three: Eight-Year-Old Jennifer

Problem Overview

Jennifer's mother brought Jennifer to see the counselor because of Jennifer's anxiety about bad things happening to the family. This began last year when they were staying in a hotel where the fire alarm went off during the night. Although the fire was minor and no one was injured, this is when the problem began. Later in the summer, Jennifer was staying with her elderly grandmother and a tornado touched down nearby. According to Jennifer, she and her grandmother had gone to a storm cellar, but when they tried to get out they were not strong enough to push the door open and were trapped there for a short while until a neighbor happened to come by. In addition to these two concerns, she worried about being in a car accident.

Other than this anxiety, Jennifer is a well-adjusted child with lots of friends. She does well in school and presents no problem at home except typical sibling conflict.

Developmental Considerations

It is not uncommon for children this age to overgeneralize about situations and imagine the worst (Bernard & Joyce, 1984). At the same time, it is important to take their worries seriously and devise concrete ways to help them come to their own conclusions and reduce the level of intensity of the worry.

Assessment

Jennifer was a very verbal child, thus it was not difficult for her to describe her fears. To get a specific assessment of the intensity of the anxiety and the frequency with which it occurred, the counselor gave her three charts marked with the days of the week. For each worry, she was to mark a 1–10 (low to high) each day. During the next visit, they discussed the degree of worry, which was higher for the accidents because they were in a car daily, and for the storms because the weather had been changeable. To determine the specific thoughts about each of these fears, the counselor asked this young client to make a list of all the things she thought about in relation to each. For storms, she listed the following: a tornado would destroy their home, bad lightening would set their house on fire, or high winds would knock trees into their house. For the car accident, Jennifer listed herself and family members being seriously hurt or one or more of them dying in a crash.

Intervention

In this case, the counselor gave Jennifer a chart and asked her to watch the weather portion of the news each night. She was supposed to note the following based on her observations: was the following day going to be (a) sunny and pleasant; (b) cloudy, but no rain; (c) rainy, but no storms; (d) windy and rainy; (e) high winds, rain, lightening, and thunder; or (f) tornado. When she and the counselor discussed the information, Jenny was able to see that there had been no bad storms all week. To see if this was more of an exception than a rule, Jennifer charted the weather for several weeks to help her see there only had been severe weather very occasionally. She and the counselor also researched tornados in the encyclopedia, discussing the rare combination of circumstances needed to produce them. She learned to use self-talk (the weather is not horribly bad very often; instead of being upset all the time, I can learn what to do in case of a tornado; I can keep reminding myself that a bad storm does not mean there will be a tornado) to reinforce the idea that although bad things can happen, it is not necessary to worry every day. To deal with the other two worries, the counselor used a similar strategy. She had Jennifer interview her father, who sold car insurance, about the number of serious accidents compared with more minor ones; and read the newspaper to chart occurrences of fires, and interview the fire chief. Several empowerment strategies also were used: Jennifer and her family purchased additional smoke alarms and bought fire extinguishers for the house.

Evaluation

Although this was not a problem that disappeared overnight, these concrete strategies helped this 8-year-old learn how to put her worries in perspective and reduce the anxiety with self-talk and fact finding.

Problem Four: Nine-Year-Old Carrie

Problem Overview

Carrie asked to see the school counselor, because, in her words, she was "scared to death to take tests." The counselor learned from the teacher that Carrie was a good student, but became extremely anxious prior to and during a test, to the point where she sometimes missed school on the day of the test or felt sick to her stomach at school as test time approached. Although she normally did quite well, Carrie was very self-critical about all her work. She was particularly hard on herself if she did not perform up to her standards on an exam. Carrie and her older brother have been living with their mother since their parents' divorce 5 years ago. They have very little contact with their father, but seem to have adjusted to the situation, according to the mother. She indicated that Carrie does not experience anxiety about anything else. She is a happy child with lots of friends.

Developmental Considerations

Many children in this stage of development are very self-critical as they become more aware of their abilities and compare them to others' (Newman & Newman, 1991). Test anxiety is not unusual, but early intervention is important.

Assessment

Because Carrie referred herself and wanted help with the problem, she had no difficulty verbalizing what she was experiencing. The problem began this year, because she received letter grades for the first time as a fourth grader. According to Carrie, she gets nervous about doing her homework well, but, because she has plenty of time to do it and check it over, it is not the same as taking a test under time pressure. To get a more comprehensive picture, the counselor asked Carrie to describe the following: (a) what she is thinking prior to taking the test, (b) what she is feeling physically prior to taking the test, (c) what she imagines will happen, and (d) how she feels emotionally. The counselor also had Carrie discuss what it is like for her during the test, and what she has tried to do to solve the problem.

Intervention

To help Carrie, the counselor used several relaxation exercises from *The Second Centering Book* (Hendricks & Roberts, 1977) to help her relax before the test. She also gave her eight test-taking tips written on index cards that could be taped inside her desk (Sycamore, Corey, & Coker, 1990). In addition, she taught Carrie to use rational disputation techniques by explaining the concept of self-talk (Bernard & Joyce, 1984). This involves mentally asking yourself questions such as, "If you try your hardest, how badly do you think you will do? Even if you don't do well, does that mean you are dumb? If you get a bad grade, what does that mean?" The counselor and Carrie practiced this technique by pretending the counselor was Carrie's friend and verbalizing fears about taking a test. Carrie responded as she would if a friend talked to her about this. An example of this procedure follows:

Counselor playing the friend: "I know I'll fail this test."

Carrie's response: "If you studied you'll probably do fine."

Counselor: "If I get a bad grade on this test, people will think I'm dumb."

Carrie: "You're not dumb even if you get a bad grade."

Following this activity, they discussed the likelihood of Carrie getting horrible grades on the tests, what her past performance had been, and what it said about her if she did not do as well as she expected. This helped her develop a more realistic view of the situation.

Evaluation

Using a combination of intervention techniques to address different dimensions of the problem was helpful in this case, but test anxiety is difficult to deal with at this age, because it is coupled with the self-critical nature of the child who is just beginning to assess strengths and weaknesses. For these interventions to be effective, the relaxation and rational disputation techniques needed to be implemented just prior to each test-taking situation, with discussion afterward about how Carrie had done, how she felt, what she did to help herself feel less anxious, and what she could do in the future if she continued to feel nervous about taking tests.

Problem Five: Eleven-Year-Old Antonio

Problem Overview

This young boy was referred to the counselor because, 6 months ago, he had been in a serious car accident, which resulted in the amputation of his right arm. His mother and stepfather indicated that initially he adjusted quite well, but suddenly he was displaying a lot of anger and would explode at the slightest provocation. As an only child, Antonio was encouraged to participate in activities such as scouting and team sports, but he had withdrawn from those and even had declined his annual visit to his father's house.

Developmental Considerations

Eleven-year-olds are more aware of their bodies (Ames, Ilg, & Baker, 1988), more self-critical (Ruble et al. 1980), and their self-concepts are influenced easily by peers (Harter, 1982). A child with a disability that makes him or her different has a high risk of being depressed (Rodgers, Hillemeier, O'Neill, & Slonim, 1981).

Assessment

Antonio was a reluctant client. The counselor worked hard to establish the relationship, letting Antonio set the pace. As is often the case, the counselor sensed this young client's anger was masking vulnerable feelings, such as fear about the implications of the loss and probable depression. Because this child seemed so skittish about counseling, the counselor decided not to use a formal depression inventory with him, but orally asked for his response to several questions to get a sense of the depression (Rutter, Izard, & Read, 1986): Was he moody? Did he feel irritable or was he easily annoyed? Did he feel dumb, worthless, or useless? Was he having trouble sleeping or was he sleeping more? Was he withdrawing from friends and usual activities? She also discussed this in length with the parents, and concluded that there was some change in his behavior and his mood was somewhat depressed, as would be expected in this situation. The counselor indicated to the parents that if the depression did not improve following intervention, medication might be needed as well.

Because Antonio volunteered very little, the counselor was more directive with him, explaining through concrete examples the feelings associated with loss: anger, loneliness, fright, sadness, denial, helplessness (Glass, 1991). Knowing that he liked to draw, she gave him sheets of paper labeled with each of these words and invited him to draw how he felt or what he was thinking or worrying about in response to any of them. This assessment activity was very enlightening. Antonio very graphically portrayed himself sitting on the sidelines while his friends played ball, getting bad grades in school because he couldn't write well with his left hand, being teased by peers for having one arm, and looking different than others.

Intervention

Taking the lead from his drawings, the counselor asked Antonio if he could talk more about having to sit on the sidelines while his friends played ball. He told her that kids with one arm cannot play baseball or other sports. The counselor suggested to him that they do some research on this, and they spent time looking through sports magazines to find baseball players with one arm. When they did, Antonio and the counselor made a list of questions he had about how to get along with this disability and they sent it to the player, who eventually responded. The counselor also gave him the book *Good Answers to Tough Questions About Physical Disabilities* (Berry, 1990), which explains how to function with a physical disability.

An adaptation of the activities *Just Different* (Vernon, 1989) and *Performance Wheel* (Vernon, 1989) were used to help Antonio learn that just because he had this disability did not mean he could not do anything; and that even though he was different in some ways, this did not mean he was worthless. Because he was not very verbal, the counselor encouraged Antonio to continue drawing to vent his angry feelings.

Evaluation

Adjusting to a disability can be a long-term process. In Antonio's case, a combination of supportive counseling and direct intervention to help him accept the disability was essential. In addition, it was important to work with Antonio's parents to help them deal with his anger and worthlessness, as well as their own concerns and issues of acceptance.

OTHER TYPICAL DEVELOPMENTAL PROBLEMS

In addition to the problems previously identified, a sampling of typical concerns children at this age experience is listed (Youngs, 1985). Some of them are so common that it might not even occur to adults that children worry about them. Unfortunately, adults often take for granted that children easily can handle some of these seemingly minor things that trouble them, forgetting that they may not always think logically enough to pull the pieces together, despite the fact that their cognitive skills are more fully developed with each passing year. Knowledge of these issues increases the sensitivity of parents and professionals, helping them anticipate problems to help children deal with them before they become full-blown concerns.

The following problems are sources of stress, listed in order of intensity and followed by behavior that may alert parents and professionals to the concern.

First Grade

Fear of riding the bus (tries to persuade parents to drive him or her to school); fear of wetting in class (overly concerned about many things; overly focused on "what if" consequences); fear of teacher disapproval (dependent behavior and constantly seeking approval); fear of being ridiculed by classmates and older students in the school (withdrawal and lack of desire to go to school); fear of receiving the first report card and not passing to second grade (high degree of negative self-talk and low self-esteem).

Second Grade

Frequently missing parents and wanting to be home with them (asks to stay home); fear of not being able to understand a lesson (cries, inattentive, anxious); not being asked to be the teacher's "helper" (seeks positive or negative attention from teacher); afraid of being disciplined by the teacher (no eye contact with teacher); afraid of being different from others in dress, appearance (feels disliked).

Third Grade

Being chosen last on any team (verbally expresses that the game is stupid or that he or she does not want to play; absences on physical education days); parent conferences ("forgets" to deliver notice about parent conferences); fear of peer disapproval or not being liked by the teacher (complains about being excluded); fear of test taking or not having time to complete work (procrastination or avoidance; absent for tests; careless work); staying after school (hurries to get work done).

Fourth Grade

Being chosen last on any team (denies wanting to play); peer disapproval of appearance, dress (indecisive about what to wear; angry if parent makes suggestions); fear of losing a friend (jealous and possessive); fear of ridicule by other students (calls names back); fear of not being liked by the teacher (frequently associates with teacher).

Fifth Grade

Fear of being chosen last on a team (pretends not to want to play); fear of losing a "best friend" (jealous and possessive); fear of not being able to complete schoolwork (careless; procrastinates); fear of peer disapproval (adamant about selecting own clothing, activities, friends); fear of not passing to sixth grade (frequently talks about grades, passing).

Sixth Grade

Fear of being chosen last on a team (denies wanting to play); fear of the unknown in terms of sexuality (jokes about it, shares myths or information); fear of not passing to junior high, middle school (increased effort or more procrastination); fear of peer disapproval of appearance (more attentive to appearance; experimentation with hair, clothes); fear of being unpopular (keeps a close friend, but cultivates several).

SUMMARY

In this chapter, several problems typical for the middle-aged child were described: anxiety about performance, developing appropriate behavioral control, and anxiety about disaster affecting the family. Helping professionals not only need to know these are commonly experienced issues, but also must be able to adjust assessment procedures to determine the exact nature of the problem and work closely with the parent(s) if possible in both the assessment and intervention process. Problems exemplified by Stevie and Antonio are not characteristic of normal developmental problems, but may be experienced by children at some point in their childhood. It is important for the practitioner to apply knowledge of developmental theory in conceptualizing the problem, the assessment procedure, and the intervention strategies with these types of issues.

Although these middle childhood years are a time of relatively stable growth, there are important developmental tasks to be mastered. In addition, an increasing number of children are faced with stressors resulting from family and environmental issues over which they have little control. Growing up is a challenge, but sensitive professionals can make a difference for children by assisting them in preventing and resolving problems.

REFERENCES

Ames, L. B., & Haber, C. C. (1985). *Your ten- to fourteen-year-old: Life in a minor key*. New York: Dell.

Ames, L. B., Ilg, F. L., & Baker, S. M. (1988). New York: Delacorte Press.

Bedford, S. (1974). *Instant replay*. New York: Institute for Rational Living.

Berger, K., & Thompson, R. (1991). *The developing child*. New York: Harper-Collins.

Bernard, M., & Joyce, M. (1984). *Rational–emotive therapy with children and adolescents*. New York: Wiley.

Berndt, T. (1981). Relations between social cognition, nonsocial cognition, and social behavior: The case of friendship. In J. H. Flavell & L. D. Ross (Eds.), *Social cognitive development: Frontiers and possible futures* (pp. 233–287). Cambridge: Cambridge University Press.

Berndt, T. (1992). *Child development*. Orlando, FL: Harcourt Brace Jovanovich.

Berry, J. (1990). *Good answers to tough questions about physical disabilities*. New York: Children's Press.

Carroll, J., & Steward, M. (1984). The role of cognitive development in children's understanding of their own feelings. *Child Development, 55*, 1486–1492.

Colangelo, N., & Dettmann, D. F. (1985). Characteristics of moral problems and solutions formed by students in grades 3–8. *Elementary School Guidance and Counseling, 19*, 260–271.

Collins, W. A. (Ed.). (1984). *Development during middle childhood*. Washington, DC: National Academy Press.

Cooney, E. W., & Selman, R. L. (1980). Children's use of social conceptions: Toward a dynamic model of social cognition. *Personnel and Guidance Journal, 58*, 344–352.

Cunningham, B., & Hare, J. (1989). Essential elements of a teacher in-service program on child bereavement. *Elementary School Guidance and Counseling, 23*, 175–182.

DePaola, T. (1973). *Nana upstairs, Nana downstairs*. Bergenfield, NJ: Penguin.

Dreikurs, R., & Grey, L. (1970). *A parents' guide to child discipline*. New York: Hawthorne.

Dustin, D., & Ehly, S. (1992). School consultation in the 1990s. *Elementary School Guidance and Counseling, 26*, 165–175.

Dweck, C. S., & Elliott, E. S. (1983). Achievement motivation. In P. H. Mussen (Ed.), *Handbook of child psychology: Vol. 4. Socialization and personality development* (pp. 643–691). New York: Wiley.

Elkind, D. (1988). *The hurried child: Growing up too fast too soon.* Reading, MA: Addison-Wesley.

Fadely, J., & Hosler, V. (1980). *Developmental psychometrics: A resourcebook for mental health workers and educators.* Springfield, IL: Charles C. Thomas.

Fischer, K. W., & Bullock, D. (1984). Cognitive development in school-age children: Conclusions and new directions. In W. A. Collins (Ed.), *Development during middle childhood: The years from six to twelve* (pp. 70–146). Washington, DC: National Academy Press.

Flavell, J. H. (1985). *Cognitive development* (2nd ed.). Englewood Cliffs, NJ: Prentice-Hall.

Furman, E. (1984). Children's patterns in mourning the death of a loved one. In H. Wass & C. Corr (Eds.), *Childhood and death* (pp. 185–202). Washington, DC: Hemisphere.

Glass, J. C. (1991). Death, loss, and grief among middle school children: Implications for the school counselor. *Elementary School Guidance and Counseling, 26,* 139–148.

Gould, D. L. (1987). *Grandpa's slide show.* New York: Lothrop, Lee, & Shepard.

Harter, S. (1982). The perceived competence scale for children. *Child Development, 53,* 87–97.

Harter, S. (1983). Developmental perspectives on the self-system. In P. H. Mussen (Series Ed.) & E. M. Heatherington (Vol. Ed.), *Handbook of child psychology: Vol.4. Socialization, personality, and social development* (pp. 275–385). New York: Wiley.

Hartup, W. W. (1983). Peer relations. In P. H. Mussen (Series Ed.) & E. M. Heatherington (Vol. Ed.), *Handbook of child psychology: Vol.4. Socialization, personality, and social development* (pp. 103–196). New York: Wiley.

Hartup, W. W. (1984). The peer context in middle childhood. In W. A. Collins (Ed.), *Development during middle childhood: The years from six to twelve* (pp. 240–282). Washington, DC: National Academy Press.

Hawes, D. (1989). Communication between teachers and children: A counselor consultant/trainer model. *Elementary School Guidance and Counseling, 24,* 58–67.

Hendricks, G., & Roberts, T. B. (1977). *The second centering book: More awareness activities for children, parents, and teachers.* Englewood Cliffs, NJ: Prentice-Hall.

Lowrey, G. H. (1986). *Growth and development of children* (8th ed.). Chicago, IL: Year Book Medical Publishers.

Marcus, H., & Nurius, P. (1984). Self-understanding and self-regulation in middle childhood. In W. A. Collins (Ed.), *Development during middle childhood: The years from six to twelve* (pp. 147–183). Washington, DC: National Academy Press.

Mathias, C. E. (1992). Touching the lives of children: Consultative interventions that work. *Elementary School Guidance and Counseling, 26,* 190–201.

Newman, B. M., & Newman, P. R. (1991). *Development through life: A psychosocial approach.* Pacific Grove, CA: Brooks/Cole.

Piaget, J. (1967). *Six psychological studies.* New York: Random House.

Rando, T. (1984). *Grief, dying and death: Clinical interventions for caregivers.* Champaign, IL: Research Press.

Rodgers, B., Hillemeier, M., O'Neill, E., & Slonim, M. (1981). Depression in the chronically ill or handicapped school-aged child. *American Journal of Maternal Child Nursing, 6,* 266–273.

Ruble, D., Boggiano, A., Feldman, N., & Loebl, J. (1980). A developmental analysis of the role of social comparison in self-evaluation. *Developmental Psychology, 16,* 105–115.

Rutter, M., Izard, C. E., & Read, P. (1986). *Depression in young people: Developmental and clinical perspectives.* New York: Guilford.

Santrock, J., & Yussen, S. (1992). *Child development: An introduction.* Dubuque, IA: William C. Brown.

Selman, R. (1971). The relation of role taking to the development of moral judgment in children. *Child Development, 42,* 79–91.

Stipek, D. (1984). Sex differences in children's attributions of success and failure on math and spelling tests. *Sex Roles, 2,* 969–981.

Sycamore, J. E., Corey, A. L., & Coker, D. H. (1990). Reducing test anxiety. *Elementary School Guidance and Counseling, 24,* 231–233.

Thompson, C. L., & Rudolph, L. B. (1992). *Counseling children.* Pacific Grove, CA: Brooks/Cole.

Vernon, A. (1989). *Thinking, feeling, behaving: An emotional education curriculum for children.* Champaign, IL: Research Press.

Walker, L. J., & Taylor, J. H. (1991). Family interaction and the development of moral reasoning. *Child Development, 62,* 264–283.

Youngs, B. B. (1985). *Stress in children.* New York: Arbor House.

CHAPTER VI

EARLY ADOLESCENCE: ASSESSMENT AND INTERVENTION

"Struggling toward maturity" is an appropriate way to describe adolescents as they move from childhood to adulthood (Bireley & Genshaft, 1991, p. 1), but it certainly does not convey all that is involved in the transition. I have vivid memories of the dichotomies characteristic of this period: receiving a teddy bear and a transistor radio for my 14th birthday, painstakingly packing away my dolls with some regret, and being kissed on the cheek in the back row of the movie theater. In *The Diary of a Young Girl* (Frank, 1963), Anne Frank so aptly captured the essence of early adolescence as she wrote,

> Yesterday I read an article . . . it might have been addressed to me personally . . . about a girl in the years of puberty who becomes quiet within and begins to think about the wonders that are happening to her body. I experience that, too, and that is why I get the feeling lately of being embarrassed about Margot, Mummy, and Daddy. . . . I think what is happening to me is so wonderful, and not only what can be seen on my body, but all that is taking place inside. (p. 115)

Schave and Schave (1989) characterized early adolescence as "a distinct and qualitatively different developmental phase" (p. xi). These authors indicated that the dramatic changes in cognition and the intensification of affect contribute to a fluctuating sense of self, and it is not until adolescence proper that self-integration actually occurs. In contrast to the typical view of early adolescence as one of "storm and stress," the Schaves view this period as part of a normal, healthy developmental process in which "quantum leaps" in cognitive functioning have a dramatic impact on development.

Early adolescence begins at about age 11 for girls, but somewhat later for boys, lasting until age 14 for girls, and slightly longer for boys (Schave & Schave, 1989). Rapid mood fluctuations characterize this period, with the adolescent shifting from intense sadness to anger to excitement to depression in a brief time. This emotional disequilibrium is accompanied by egocentrism, pubertal changes, and an increased need for independence. Ambivalent feelings accompany this struggle for autonomy. Although it may appear as if early adolescents no longer need their parents, they still continue to require their support in setting limits, providing structure, and being emotionally available (Colten & Gore, 1991; Schave & Schave, 1989). This can be very confusing to parents: the adolescent may be loving one minute and hostile the next, with tantrum-like behavior similar to that of a toddler.

As they shift to formal operational thinking, adolescents are psychologically vulnerable and experience a loss of control over their affect (Schave & Schave, 1989). As a result, they are self-absorbed and ambivalent. Teachers and parents may compare this period to riding on a roller coaster with a great deal of unpredictability in moods and behavior.

According to several researchers (Klimek & Anderson, 1989; LeFrancois, 1992; Powers, Hauser, & Kilner, 1989), 70%–75% of teenagers negotiate this phase without extreme difficulty, whereas 25%–30% resort to delinquency, acting out, drug dependence, school failure, sexual promiscuity, and other self-destructive behaviors. Klimek and Anderson (1989) noted that boys tend to "act out" and girls tend to "act in," experiencing more powerful mood swings, depression, and low self-esteem.

CHARACTERISTICS OF THE EARLY ADOLESCENT

Early adolescence is a frustrating developmental stage for teenagers and their parents. The hormonal, pubertal, social, and physical changes contribute to their emotional upheaval and often result in defensive, ultrasensitive, and temperamental behavior (Schave & Schave, 1989). Parents and professionals working with early adolescents often misinterpret the defensiveness and temperamental behavior and fail to see how this masks vulnerability, in part because the teenagers send mixed messages. As a result, parents frequently overreact to these overt behaviors and symptoms, which results in conflict and misguided attempts to deal effectively with children at this age.

Following are descriptions of early adolescence in terms of self, social, cognitive, physical, emotional, and moral development. These developmental characteristics can assist professionals in appropriate assessment and intervention.

Self-Development

Self-integration is one of the critical developmental tasks of early adolescence (Dusek, 1991; Schave & Schave, 1989). Ironically, as these youth strive for self-integration, they also show increased dependency, which creates ambivalent feelings toward parents. Schave and Schave, as well as Elkind (1984), were concerned that although early adolescents push for autonomy, they are still immature and lack life experiences. These contrasts, coupled with teenagers' cognitive, physical, pubertal, and social changes, leave them very vulnerable, with no strong core sense of self.

During this period of development, it is not unusual for young adolescents to be very egocentric: they see themselves as more important than they really are, or feel that no one else experiences things the way they do (Berger & Thompson, 1991). Closely linked to this egocentrism is the "time warp" concept, adolescents' inability to link events, situation, and feelings together to form a comprehensive sense of their own "history." For example, they are unwilling to accept that their behavior influences whether they will be able to go out with friends on Saturday night, or the idea that because they did not study they got a bad grade (Schave & Schave, 1989). Schave and Schave maintained that if early adolescents connected these events, they would feel guilt, shame, or anger. Because they become overwhelmed by these feelings, they tend to dissociate feelings from events and place responsibility for problems away from themselves.

Early adolescents are also very self-conscious. They assume that everyone is looking at them or thinking about them. Elkind (1984, 1988) attributed this to the concept of the "imaginary audience," the belief that others are as concerned with us as we are. As a result of the imaginary audience, early adolescents fantasize about how others will react to them. Thus, they become supersensitive and overly concerned with their performance and appearance, or they become vain and conceited. According to Elkind and Bowen (1979), girls are more concerned with the imaginary audience than boys, as are delinquent boys compared with nondelinquents of either gender (Anolik, 1981). Accompanying the self-consciousness is a decrease in self-esteem (Baumrind, 1987).

Elkind (1974) also described the "invincibility fable," a belief in one's invulnerability. In essence, this fable contributes to the notion that, because of "my" uniqueness, bad things may happen to others, but not to "me." For example, teenagers' friends may get pregnant, but they will not; they can take risks, because they will not get caught; they can take drugs, but they will not become addicted. Closely tied to this is the "personal fable" (Elkind, 1984), in which adolescents imagine their lives as heroic or special. They might see themselves becoming world-famous rock stars or destined for fortune and fame.

Generally by age 13, egocentrism peaks, but it is not until several years later that it declines enough for adolescents to feel more at ease with themselves and in social situations (Elkind & Bowen, 1979; Pesce &

Harding, 1986). Although the "search for self" begins during early adolescence, it is not until mid-adolescence that full integration is achieved.

Social Development

As early adolescents move away from their families, peers play a dominant role and are a vital part of the growing up process (Berndt, 1989). While they become more involved with peers and see them as a source of support, adolescents are extremely sensitive and vulnerable to peer humiliation (Johnson & Kottman, 1992; Schave & Schave, 1989). The imaginary audience contributes to this sensitivity, because adolescents see themselves as the center of attention, but fear disapproval, judgment, or put-downs. To protect against this, they choose peers who are equal and similar. Often they dress alike, use the same idiosyncracies in their speech, and develop "rules" about what topics to discuss or which activities to pursue (Klimek & Anderson, 1989).

As children get older, their friendships become increasingly more intimate; and by early adolescence, a friend is described as "someone who understands your feelings, makes you feel better when you're 'down,' and who knows almost everything there is to know about you" (Berndt, 1992, p. 495). Adolescents distinguish between friends and acquaintances, and use the term *best friend* only for someone with whom they have a very close relationship (Berndt, 1992; Selman, 1980). Adolescent friendships are more emotionally bonding and stable than they were in childhood (Sarafino & Armstrong, 1986). Intimate friendships are more prevalent for girls than for boys, and boys are less likely to disclose personal information, because they might be teased or ridiculed (Youniss & Smollar, 1985).

During adolescence, more complex social relationships develop due primarily to two factors: norms and standards of conduct, and association by reputation. For example, adolescents may be a "jock," a "dirthead," or a "preppie," assuming the behavior and image that they go along with a particular group. They also may be part of a clique or gang and adopt the norms and standards of this group. In either situation, peer pressure becomes a salient issue, accompanied by both positive and negative aspects.

Although adolescent egocentrism can negatively affect the teenager's ability to learn about others' feelings and motives, social experience helps reduce this (Sarafino & Armstrong, 1986). As they grow cognitively, they are better able to consider the listener's point of view and understand how their perceptions of people may contradict what others think (Selman, 1980).

Between the ages of 11 and 13, early adolescents tend to have more negative than positive feelings about the opposite gender, depending on when pubertal changes occur, which affect when sexual interest begins (Berger & Thompson, 1991). They typically enter dating relationships gradually as a group of young females associates with a group of young males, although some adolescents date infrequently at this age.

Cognitive Development

A shift from concrete to formal operational thinking occurs in early adolescence, resulting in what Schave and Schave (1989) considered "the most drastic and dramatic change in cognition that occurs in anyone's life" (p. 7). These authors noted that formal operational thinking begins at about age 11, but is not attained until at least age 15–20. As early adolescents move into this realm, they begin to think more abstractly and can hypothesize. They also tend to idealize and compare themselves and others to these ideal standards (Berger & Thompson, 1991).

With an increased ability to use abstract thinking comes an ability to think more logically, although, as Berger and Thompson (1991) noted, adolescents do not always apply this logic to themselves. Newman and Newman (1991) identified the following new conceptual skills that accompany formal operational thought:

1. Adolescents are able to mentally manipulate more than two categories of variables simultaneously. They can consider how much they would have to save per month and for how long to buy a compact disc player.
2. They have the ability to think about future changes. For example, they are able to see how their relationship with their parents will be different in 10 years.
3. They can hypothesize about the logical sequence of events, thus being able to see that their behavior on the job influences their ability to keep that job.
4. They can predict consequences of actions, understanding that if they skip school repeatedly they could be expelled.
5. They can detect logical consistency or inconsistency in statements. For instance, they can see that, despite that there are laws against discrimination it still occurs in practice.
6. They understand that they are expected to act in certain ways, because of the norms of their family, culture, or community, but they realize that the norms may be different in other cultures, communities, or families.

In comparing this list to early adolescents you know, you may see discrepancies between what is and what is supposed to occur conceptually at this period of development. It is important to note considerable variability exists in the way early adolescents think. According to Strahan (1983), only about one in three eighth graders is a formal operational thinker. Variation also occurs in the degree to which they use formal operational thinking consistently. For example, it is not uncommon to find an early adolescent who uses formal operational thinking to solve math problems, but does not use it when reasoning about interpersonal relationships (Santrock & Yussen, 1992). Because of this variability in applying formal operational thinking, it can be confusing to work with early adolescents.

Physical Development

Except during infancy, physical changes occur more rapidly during adolescence than at any other point in the life span (Dusek, 1991). At about age 11 for females and 13 for males, increased production of sex hormones occurs and changes associated with puberty begin: maturation of the reproductive system and the appearance of secondary sex characteristics (pubic hair, breast enlargement, and voice change). A growth spurt also occurs, with increases in weight and height and a redistribution of body tissue and proportions. This growth spurt lasts for about 3 years, but begins approximately 2 years earlier in girls than in boys (Malina, 1991; Sarafino & Armstrong, 1986). The rate of development for both males and females varies considerably, which affects early adolescents in several ways (Newman & Newman, 1991). First, physical growth affects their ability to perform certain tasks. For example, teenagers may be uncoordinated, because the size of their hands or feet is disproportionate to other body parts. Second, physical development influences the way others perceive them. Adults may comment on how they have grown and how different they look, which may embarrass or please them. Third, it affects the way they see themselves. Early adolescents are painfully aware of being more or less mature than peers, developing "locker room phobia," because they do not want peers to see their bodies. Because there is so much discontinuity in the rate of pubertal change, early adolescents may be less physically attractive during this period, when they are so preoccupied with how they look (Baumrind, 1987).

Because adolescents vary so tremendously in their rate of physical maturity, this can be one of the most difficult periods of development. Early maturers tend to be more socially mature, more active in school affairs, self-confident, and more athletic than late maturers (Tobin-

Richards, Boxer, & Petersen, 1983). At the same time, Newman and Newman (1991) contended that young women who menstruate early feel embarrassed by their femininity and are reluctant to discuss their physical changes with peers. According to Sarafino and Armstrong (1986), late maturing adolescents often feel socially inadequate and frustrated by their rate of development. They feel more self-conscious and worry about being teased or disliked. It appears that the rate of maturation is a "mixed bag" that creates anxiety for both males and females (Newman & Newman, 1991).

Females first develop breast buds and pubic and underarm hair, followed by changes in the vagina, clitoris, and uterus. Females generally experience their first menstruation between ages 10 and 16, depending on their weight and amount of body fat (Frisch, 1991). After the first menstruation, it usually takes 12–18 months for females to become fertile (Sarafino & Armstrong, 1986).

In males, the beginning of sexual maturity occurs earlier than the growth spurt by about 1 year. At about age 12, the testes and scrotum enlarge and pubic hair develops. In the following year, the penis begins to grow and continues to enlarge for at least 2 more years. Underarm and facial hair appear at about age 14. Internal sex organ changes also begin to develop, and by age 14 to 15 boys are capable of ejaculating, although the sperm count is low and they are not fertile until a year later (Sarafino & Armstrong, 1986). During this period, males experience nocturnal emissions (Newman & Newman, 1991).

As several authors noted, the physical changes occurring in early adolescence have psychological meaning as well, which often results in ambivalence (Berger & Thompson, 1991; Newman & Newman, 1991; Sarafino & Armstrong, 1986). These changes, accompanied by the dramatic shift in cognitive development, have a major impact on young teenagers.

Emotional Development

Early adolescence includes great emotional variability and moodiness, often accompanied by emotional outbursts (Newman & Newman, 1991). Negative emotional states such as moodiness and apathy are experienced more frequently (Larson & Lampman-Petraitis, 1989), along with troublesome emotions: anxiety, shame, depression, embarrassment, guilt, shyness, and anger (Adelson & Doehrman, 1980). It commonly is assumed that the increase in negative emotions can be attributed to the hormonal changes associated with puberty, but several authors have found a minimal relationship between negative affect and hormonal status (Brooks-Gunn & Warren, 1989; Santrock, 1987). Others have posited that stressful events contribute to negative emotion, or that it is more of an ecological issue, because adolescents spend more time away from the family than do preadolescents, and being alone often is associated with a lower mood (Colten & Gore, 1991). It may be that each of these is a contributing factor.

As they shift from concrete to more abstract and hypothetical thinking, early adolescents are better able to see discrepancies between the real and the ideal, the expected and the actual. However, these insights frequently result in disappointment (Larsen & Asmussen, 1991). Early adolescents also are more aware of others' feelings and thoughts. Consequently, they are more sensitive to the ups and downs associated with social interactions, often overreacting to who said what about whom. Weiner and Graham (1984) contended that cognitive development from childhood to adolescence opens the door to new emotions such as guilt, shame, anxiety, depression, and anger, and that adolescents feel increasingly more vulnerable. Males and females respond differently to their heightened awareness of negative feelings: females are more emotionally expressive and more sensitive to the emotional states of others (Bukatko & Daehler, 1992). They also experience more shame, guilt, and depression. These feelings are more likely to be caused by problems in interpersonal relationships (Larsen & Asmussen, 1991). On the other hand, males are more activity based and external, experiencing more anger and contempt, which are not as closely tied to social interaction (Larsen & Asmussen, 1991; Ostrov, Offer, & Howard, 1989).

Because they experience a wider range of emotions, a major task for early adolescents is developing tolerance for their emotionality, rather than feeling ashamed of their feelings or afraid they are "going crazy" (Newman & Newman, 1991). If this does not happen, they may overcontrol their emotions, which can result in less emotional expression, greater submissiveness, and timidity. Or they may undercontrol, which leads to impulsive reactions and some type of delinquent behavior (Gold & Petronio, 1980; Strober, 1981).

The increased intensity of emotions permeates all aspects of early adolescents' lives and makes this a challenging time for early adolescents and their families.

Moral Development

Most early adolescents are in what Kohlberg termed *the conventional level of morality*: they understand and accept the social norms for their behavior (Berndt, 1992). More specifically, the majority identify with Stage 3, interpersonal normative morality. Adolescents at this stage believe that people should act like others expect them to act. For example, a friend should be loyal or a teacher should be fair. However, it is not uncommon for early adolescents to be in Stage 2, where they are able to consider more than one perspective in a given situation and recognize conflict between two people's perspectives. However, it is important to remember that these moral developmental stages may not be applicable in all cultures (Gibbs & Schnell, 1985).

Issues that present the most challenge for early adolescents in terms of moral decision making include decisions about intervening or reporting; problems with alcohol, drugs, and tobacco; relationship issues; and conflicts about cheating, stealing, honesty, and lying (Colangelo & Dettmann, 1985). These same issues were of most concern to middle-aged children.

Between the ages of 10 and 18, young people progress more in moral reasoning than at any other stage of life (Colby, Kohlberg, Gibbs, & Lieberman, 1983). However, because their moral reasoning develops in varying degrees along with their ability to think abstractly, it is important to give adolescents the opportunity to discuss moral issues and make choices that facilitate development of more complex moral decision making (Rest, 1986).

PARENTAL INVOLVEMENT WITH EARLY ADOLESCENTS

Barrish and Barrish (1989) said it is typical for early adolescents to question parental authority. However, despite that early adolescents try to scare parents away with their assertive or, at times, aggressive attempts to be independent, parents play a vital role in the early adolescents' development as an independent agent and problem solver (Baumrind, 1987; Schave & Schave, 1989). In many respects, early adolescents are like 2-year-olds who say "No, me!" But unlike toddlers, early adolescents may be more successful in getting parents to abdicate their role, leaving the 12- to14-year-olds struggling to grow up without a parental support system. Although they are reluctant to admit it, adolescents need a gradual relaxation of rules and limits so they can "try their wings" with a safety net.

Baumrind (1987) viewed the major task of early adolescence as development, but saw it as a movement away from dependence on the family to an interdependence. This author claimed that individuation does not have to imply emotional distance from parents, but rather a reorganization in which family members work together to "renegotiate and redistribute entitlements and obligations" (p. 121). Helping professionals play an important role in educating parents about early adolescent development and encouraging parents to continue to facilitate their youngsters' growing up process.

PROBLEM ASSESSMENT AND INTERVENTION: SELECTED CASE STUDIES

Early adolescents are frequently in a state of flux, on "cloud nine" one minute and "down in the dumps" the next. Although these moods are unpredictable and not easily controlled, they often are related to developmental processes, rather than circumstances in their lives (Johnson & Kottman, 1992). Of equal consideration is the fact that adolescents move through the developmental sequence at different rates, resulting in a great deal of variation in maturity levels, which impacts adolescents, their parents, and their peers in numerous ways.

In the following section, problems of the early adolescent, aged 12–14, are described. Examples of typical developmental problems and more circumstantial problems are identified, along with assessment and intervention strategies.

Problem One: Twelve-Year-Old Beth

Problem Overview

Beth sought out the school counselor because her best friend was ignoring her at times and had not spent as much time with her lately as she had in the past few months. Although Beth had other friends, she valued her relationship with Sara most. Beth became very upset when Sara went to a movie with someone else, ignored her in the lunchroom, or did things with other friends after school. According to Beth, Sara was her best friend and should not be spending time with other girls. As is typical for this age, when things were going well with Sara, Beth was elated, but when Sara drifted away, she felt like her whole world was coming apart, despite that she did well in school and had no major problems at home.

Developmental Considerations

Twelve-year-olds have a tendency to be possessive about their best friends and cannot accept readily that these friends may have other good friends. Loyalty and commitment to themselves is of utmost importance (Berger & Thompson, 1991).

Assessment

Although Beth was very verbal, she tended to ramble a lot, and the counselor thought he might get a more specific assessment if he asked her to write a short story describing the recent conflict with her best friend. As the counselor read it, he asked direct questions to determine what Beth thought about herself and about Sara when Sara did not want to participate in the same activity as Beth. He also wanted to determine how often conflicts occurred between them, how they both responded, and how Beth felt. The counselor wanted to know if Beth was angry, which would imply she thought her friend should go along with what she wanted to do; hurt; or sad, which would indicate Beth felt rejected and not "good enough" for Sara. The counselor also used a series of open-ended sentences:

1. If my best friend does not sit by me every day, it means that _____.

2. If my best friend does something with another friend, I feel _____ and think _____.

3. If my best friend says something mean to me, I feel _____ and think _____.

The combination of the story and the unfinished sentences helped the counselor understand that Beth felt helpless and more like a victim when things did not go well with Sara. She felt inadequate, rather than angry, which is an important distinction in designing an appropriate intervention to address the specific problem.

Intervention

Because Beth was internalizing, rather than externalizing, this experience, the counselor chose to focus more on Beth's concept of herself and what it said about her if a friend rejected her even temporarily. He first adapted an activity called Glad to Be Me (Vernon, 1989) to help this 12-year-old see that rejection from others does not mean she is not a good person. This activity was followed by another, *Different Types of Friends* (Vernon, 1988), to show Beth that there are different types of friends who meet different needs; friendships cannot be exclusive. He also used the book *Friendship Is Forever, Isn't It?* (Youngs, 1990) to help Beth realize friendships change. To work on her feelings of helplessness in this situation, the counselor had Beth look at her options when Sara ignored her by using a problem-solving wheel that helped Beth identify alternatives and positive and negative consequences of each (Vernon, self-developed game).

Evaluation

Because friendship issues are so pervasive for early adolescents, the problem did not go away overnight. It was necessary to work over a period of time to help Beth feel less helpless and not as vulnerable to

Sara's rejection, and then to help Beth build friendship skills with others, which was accomplished through small-group counseling.

Problem Two: Twelve-Year-Old Jeff

Problem Overview

Jeff's parents referred him to the counselor because he had refused to go to school for the last 10 days, shortly after entering seventh grade. According to the parents, this had not been a problem during elementary school. Jeff had a lot of friends and did well academically. However, this year he began complaining that he did not feel well and needed to stay home. At first they allowed this, but after several days realized that he did not seem sick and insisted that he go to school. Because Jeff did not like to ride the bus, his father dropped him off, but later in the day received a call from the school saying that Jeff had skipped his fourth hour class and left the building. Jeff's explanation to his parents was that he felt sick again. Prior to the session with the counselor, Jeff had a complete physical and was pronounced healthy.

Developmental Considerations

It is not uncommon for adolescents to be afraid of going to school, because they create the imaginary audience, fantasize about how others will react to their appearance and behavior, and overgeneralize about how "awful" they look or that everyone is looking at them (Berger & Thompson, 1991). In addition, the transition from elementary school, in terms of structure and academic expectations, can be a source of anxiety.

Assessment

Jeff was exceptionally shy and resisted talking about the school attendance problem, although he did say this school was several times larger than the elementary school and there were lots of new students from other schools. To learn more from Jeff, the counselor asked him to write his responses to these unfinished sentences.

1. When I go to school, I feel _____.
2. The part of the school day I like best is _____.
3. The part of the school day I like least is _____.
4. The subject that is easiest for me is _____.
5. The subject that is hardest for me is _____.
6. I am afraid of _____.
7. Other kids in this school _____.
8. Teachers in this school _____.

9. This year at school is different from last year, because
_____.

10. If I could change something about this school, it would be
_____.

In analyzing the responses, Jeff seemed more concerned about being made fun of in the locker room than he was about academics, although this was also a factor. In probing further, the counselor discovered this was the first year students had to dress for physical education. Because Jeff was slight and immature, the counselor hypothesized that Jeff was not as fully developed as his peers, which could result in the teasing that Jeff had expressed concern about on his assessment exercise. Furthermore, Jeff's responses indicated he was afraid of getting bad grades in school, because junior high seemed a lot harder than elementary school, the routine was confusing, and Jeff was worried about getting to the right class on time.

Intervention

To address these problems, the counselor first assured Jeff that his concerns were typical for his age and that a lot of his friends were probably experiencing similar feelings. Second, she explained the concept of the "imaginary audience" to him, followed by some "reality check" techniques.

She adapted an activity called *Magnify* (Pincus, 1990), in which several events were listed and Jeff was instructed to magnify their importance by turning them into a catastrophe. For example:

1. You walk into class late, because you could not get your locker open. Catastrophic thought: _____.
2. You go into the locker room to change for physical education. Catastrophic thought: _____.
3. You do not understand how to do an assignment. Catastrophic thought: _____.
4. You get a bad grade on your first test. Catastrophic thought: _____.

After Jeff identified the worst case scenario, the counselor taught him to look at the probable situation by adapting *Getting Straight Our Magnifications* (Pincus, 1990).

You walk into class late because you could not get your locker open:

    Best case scenario:_____.
    Worst case scenario (previous activity):_____.
    Probable scenario:_____.

By identifying best, worst, and probable outcomes for each question, Jeff began to dispute some of his anxieties about various seventh grade issues. The counselor helped him look at best and worst case and probable scenarios for not going to school, and then helped him develop self-statements to deal with his anxiety about going to school: (a) even though it seems like everyone is looking at me, in reality I know they are not; (b) if I do not understand how to do an assignment, I can ask the teacher and it does not mean I'm dumb; and (c) it is scary now to be in a bigger school, but elementary school seemed big too when I started, and I adjusted.

Jeff and the counselor drew up a contract stating that he would go to school. The counselor also invited Jeff to keep a "worry box," writing down the things he was worried about for that day and putting them in a box, then checking the box at the end of the day to see if what he had worried about actually had been a problem for him.

Evaluation

If Jeff's parents had not been aware of this problem, it easily could have become more serious. In this case, Jeff agreed to the contract, and the intervention strategies gradually helped him control the problem. Although it is not uncommon for seventh graders to have school phobic issues, it is sometimes difficult for them to identify specifically what they are avoiding. By being aware of developmental concerns, the counselor can design assessment instruments that help pinpoint the specific concerns so the anxiety can be resolved. In some cases, behavior modification techniques or desensitization also may need to be considered.

Problem Three: Thirteen-Year-Old Kara

Problem Overview

Kara, an eighth grader, was sent to counseling because her mother was concerned that she had recently begun to restrict her eating and was increasing her exercise beyond her normal participation in track, volleyball, cheerleading, and ballet. Although it did not appear to her mother that Kara had lost much weight, she was aware that if Kara continued her present behaviors, an eating disorder easily could develop. Her mother could not identify any particular event that precipitated this change in eating and exercise. There had been no recent loss or change in Kara's life, except that her older sister, who was slightly heavy and watched what she ate, was home from college over the summer. She and Kara were very close, and the mother speculated that maybe this had something to do with Kara's sudden preoccupation with food. Other than this presenting symptom, Kara had a close circle of friends, did very well in school, and seemed relatively happy at home and at school.

Developmental Considerations

Adolescents are very conscious of their appearance, and for females weight is of most concern (Simmons & Blythe, 1987). Studies show that, even in sixth grade, females are dissatisfied with their weight. Regardless of maturation status or exercise levels, girls between the ages of 14 and 16 want to be about 12 pounds lighter (Brooks-Gunn & Warren, 1989). This desire to be thin is reinforced by the media, and adolescents who fail to meet the ideal portrayed in television and advertising often feel inadequate and depressed.

Assessment

Some unhealthy eating is inevitable in adolescence, but it is important to be alert to changes, either in terms of restricting or binging. To assess the extent of Kara's problem, the counselor asked her to complete a 30-item scale adapted from an eating disorder questionnaire used by a local hospital and one developed by Akeroyd-Guillory (1988) to measure attitudes, feelings, and behaviors about food, exercise, and body image. Kara was to rate each question as: always, usually, often, sometimes, rarely, or never. Sample items included:

1. I feel satisfied with the shape of my body.
2. I think about dieting.
3. I think that I am too fat.
4. If I gain a pound, I worry that I will keep gaining.
5. I think that my stomach is too big.
6. I like the way my thighs are shaped.
7. I think about being thinner.
8. I feel guilty about eating.
9. I want to exercise a lot.
10. I feel comfortable eating in front of others.

Because people with eating disorders often do not experience a full range of feelings or distort them (Garfinkel & Garner, 1982), Kara was asked to respond in the same manner to questions relating to feelings:

1. I have trouble expressing how I feel to others.
2. I get confused about how I really feel.
3. I feel angry.

4. I get easily upset over little things.
5. I feel inadequate.

Body image is also an issue for clients with eating disorders (Orbach, 1986). To assess this, the counselor invited Kara to draw a picture of herself and a picture of herself with her family. She wanted to see how she portrayed herself in comparison to her sister and how she viewed family relationships. The counselor also asked her to respond to the following open-ended sentences to determine if Kara felt she had to be perfect to please herself or others, and how she felt about growing up, because both of these are issues with eating disorder clients (Rumney, 1983).

1. Now that I am an adolescent, I feel _____.
2. The person(s) who expect(s) the most from me is (are) _____.
3. If I were younger, I would feel _____.
4. If I disappoint my parents or teachers, I feel _____.
5. If I do not do well in school, athletics, or music activities, I feel _____.

The counselor obtained further information about Kara's eating patterns and exercise by having Kara keep a food and exercise chart. The counselor then analyzed the data and determined that, although the problem was not severe at this point, Kara was beginning to develop some unhealthy patterns based on her desire not to "be fat" like her sister. Perfectionism did not seem to be major issues, but there definitely were distorted ideas about body image that affected her self-esteem. The counselor also sensed that the mother was rather overprotective and at some level wanted to keep Kara as her "little girl," evidenced by a comment such as "Kim is in college, so all I have now is my little girl."

Intervention

The first intervention consisted of Kara looking through magazines and the counselor's collection of photographs to identify people who were skinny, heavy, huge, and just right. After grouping these pictures, the counselor took a polaroid shot of Kara and asked her to put her picture in one of the piles. As the counselor anticipated, Kara put her's in the "heavy" pile. To make the comparisons more relevant, she asked Kara to bring snapshots of her friends. Once again she categorized, and although it was apparent to the counselor that Kara was among the thinnest of her peers, Kara saw herself as heavier than most. The counselor then asked direct questions such as the following to help Kara develop a more realistic perspective: "Are you approximately the same height as this friend? Are your legs fatter than her's? Is your waist bigger?

Does your stomach stick out?" Because these were specific questions and not a global assessment of the entire body, Kara was more realistic in her responses. The counselor helped her see that she had answered "no" to several of the questions, and that although it might seem that she was bigger, in reality she was not.

The counselor also worked with Kara on her fear of becoming like her sister. She had Kara bring in snapshots of Kim when she was in eighth grade and compare them with snapshots of herself at present. This helped her see that, even then, Kim was larger than Kara. She also invited Kim to attend a counseling session and had Kim share data she had obtained from her doctor about healthy weight range and eating habits. In this way, Kara was able to see that she was well within the normal range for her age and height, but that Kim had been overweight even as an eighth grader.

Other interventions included making a collage by cutting out pictures of healthy versus unhealthy food choices, setting goals to eat healthy meals and exercise moderately, and reading Erlanger's (1988) book, *Eating Disorders: A Question and Answer Book About Anorexia Nervosa and Bulimia* and Alvin and Silversteins' (1991) *So You Think You're Fat?*, a book about weight and body image. The counselor also worked with Kara's mother (a single parent since Kara had been 3 months old) on letting her "little girl" grow up.

Evaluation

Although Berger and Thompson (1991) noted that treatment for eating disorders usually is successful in stopping destructive eating patterns, others (Garfinkel & Garner, 1982, 1984; Rumney, 1983) saw it as a much more complicated process. Although Kara was just beginning to restrict her eating and develop distorted images about her body, it still was difficult to dispute her sense of being too heavy and combat her fear about getting fat. Although some of the accompanying issues such as perfectionism, excessive compulsive behavior, depression, and other physiological issues had not developed yet, the fact that she was conscious of her weight was a signal that early intervention was necessary. Through a variety of cognitive–behavioral methods and work on self-image and acceptance of her body, Kara gradually stopped restricting.

Problem Four: Fourteen-Year-Old Jaime

Problem Overview

Jaime, a ninth grader, had moved to the United States from South America when he was in third grade. His parents both spoke English fluently, and aside from having less money than they had had in South America, they had adjusted well and liked living in the Midwest.

The first indication of any problem was when Jaime's grades started slipping and he was truant from school on two occasions. At home he was becoming more defiant, challenging rules, and ignoring his curfew. After he was caught smoking in the school restroom, the principal requested a conference and subsequently recommended counseling.

Developmental Considerations

As Larsen and Asmussen (1991) noted, males at this age experience anger and contempt. Their increased need for independence prompts them to take risks to assert themselves and "do as they please." This sense of entitlement often results in rebelliousness (Schave & Schave, 1989). Early adolescents also are influenced easily by peer pressure (Berndt, 1982; Newman & Newman, 1991). Their ambivalence toward parental structure and limit setting can affect how parents discipline (Schave & Schave, 1989).

Assessment

Jaime refused to attend the first counseling session, so his parents met with the counselor. The fact that they were not able to get him to counseling indicated that there also might be some parenting issues that needed to be addressed. The counselor decided to start at this point, requesting each parent to respond to questions such as the following by circling always, sometimes, or never on each item:

1. We agree on rules for our child.
2. If our child breaks a rule, there are consequences.
3. We are consistent about enforcing consequences.
4. If our child has problems, it must mean we are bad parents.
5. It is easier to let our child do as he or she pleases than to enforce rules.
6. Getting angry is an effective way to get our child to obey.
7. If we get too firm, our child will reject us.

Based on the responses to these types of questions, the counselor verified that working with the parents on effective discipline was part of the intervention. He instructed the parents to pick Jaime up at school the following week and bring him to the appointment without informing him ahead of time, letting the counselor deal with his resistance.

Jaime was indeed resistant, informing the counselor that he did not have a problem and did not intend to talk. The counselor assured him that he understood that counseling would not be his activity of choice, but indicated that the school was concerned and that if he did not want them on his back all the time, it might be a good idea to let the counselor help him. It was apparent that Jaime felt he should be able to act as he pleased, and that no one had the right to tell him what to do.

Because this young client was not willing to talk, the counselor asked him if he could share some of the songs he listened to that were meaningful to him and why. Jaime described several, expounding that censorship was wrong and adults should not restrict kids' freedom. The counselor asked Jaime to give him examples of what he felt were reasonable rules at home and at school, to which he responded that he did not think there should be any. Asked if his friends had rules at home, he insisted that they did not, implying that even though he did, he never paid attention to them and usually his parents just threatened to ground him, but did not follow through.

The counselor learned from his parents that Jaime had been an above-average student prior to this year. When asked about his declining grades, Jaime said he did not like most of his subjects and he had better things to do with his time.

Although depression in adolescents often is masked by anger, Jaime's eating and sleeping patterns were normal, and he described himself as being happy as long as adults "keep off my case"; there was no indication of self-destructive behavior. When asked if he ever felt depressed, Jaime replied, "Only when my parents keep on me."

Intervention

After assessing the situation, the counselor thought this was a rather typical case of adolescent rebellion that could get worse without intervention, for both Jaime and his parents. He first worked with the parents to dispute their belief that it is easier to give in than to follow through with discipline by having them read *Surviving and Enjoying Your Adolescent* (Barrish & Barrish, 1989). This book normalizes the adolescent quest for independence and helps parents understand that they can tolerate their own discomfort if their child is upset with them for imposing rules. The counselor explained the importance of parental consistency and adolescents' need for limits, instructing them on the use of logical consequences (Dreikurs & Grey, 1970), and invited them to read *Stop Struggling with Your Teen* (Weinhaus & Friedman, 1988), a practical book about solving parent–teen conflicts.

With Jaime, the counselor listed the problematic behaviors identified by parents and teachers: school truancy, mouthy behavior, breaking curfew, being disrespectful to parents, declining grades, and smoking. He then asked his client to write down positive and negative consequences for each problem. By looking at it in this manner, it was apparent that there were more negatives than positives. The counselor adapted "Assess the Decision" from *Thinking, Feeling, Behaving* (Vernon, 1989), which helped Jaime look at short- and long-term consequences and the effects of the decision on self and others.

The counselor also worked with Jaime to give up his demand that he always should get to do what he wanted by asking how his actions were helping him, and focused on Jaime's anger. To do this, he used an activity, *Where Feelings Come From* (Knaus, 1974), to show this young client the connection between events, thoughts, feelings, and behavior/reactions. The counselor asked Jaime to identify several situations that angered him and used the HTFR (happening, thought, feeling, behavior/reaction) format to show Jaime how his anger developed and how to change his thinking to decrease the intensity of the anger. Because Jaime's parents had some concerns about his peers, the counselor worked with the school counselor to establish a small group with some positive role models and work on the issue of rules and consequences.

Evaluation

As can be expected, once the parents agreed on rules and started to enforce consequences, the rebellion temporarily escalated. By continuing to stress to Jaime that he was choosing his consequences as a result of his behavior, Jaime's behavior improved over time. It was important to help the parents learn not to take Jaime's verbal abuse personally, but to be firm and consistent with their follow through.

Problem Five: Fourteen-Year-Old Trisha

Problem Overview

Trisha asked to see the school counselor, because she frequently felt unhappy and did not really know why. She had friends, her grades were fine, and things were all right at home, but as she tearfully explained to the counselor, "Sometimes I feel like the only one who understands me is my dog."

Developmental Considerations

Early adolescence is a confusing time, and it is not at all unusual for youngsters to have vague feelings of discontent or to feel "all alone" in their search for self. Early intervention usually is successful in preventing problems from developing into more serious concerns.

Assessment

Because Trisha could not point to any one thing that was disturbing her, the counselor used a needs assessment form, *Concerns I Have* (Strub, 1990/1991). This 50-item checklist assesses a wide variety of concerns pertaining to the early adolescent. The youngster responds to each item by identifying it as a big concern, a small concern, sometimes a concern, or not at all a concern. Sample items include:

1. I wish I could talk more in a group.
2. Other boys and girls are better than me.
3. I often feel lonesome.
4. I wish my parents understood me better.
5. I wish I had more friends.
6. I would like to change many things about myself.
7. My feelings are too easily hurt.
8. I am not doing as well in school as I can.
9. I would like to be more important to my family.
10. I wish I felt better about myself.

In looking at the results of this checklist, items of most concern seemed to fall in the category of wanting to feel better about herself and being too emotionally sensitive.

Intervention

To address the self-image issue, the counselor used several activities, including having Trisha write a commercial or design a brochure to "sell herself" (Canfield & Wells, 1976, p. 109). Trisha also completed an adjective wardrobe (Canfield & Wells, 1976), writing words that described herself on individual pieces of paper and rank ordering them from most to least pleasing. Trisha then decided which ones she wanted to expand on and which she wanted to eliminate so she could establish goals for change. In addition, the counselor used an activity called *Voicebox* (Vernon, 1989), which helped Trisha learn to utilize positive self-talk as a way to cope with self-put-downs. The counselor also encouraged Trisha to read *Why Can't Anyone Hear Me? A Guide for Surviving Adolescence* (Eichoness, 1989), which focuses on improving self-esteem.

To deal with Trisha's sense of emotional vulnerability, the counselor adapted two activities from *Feeling Good About Yourself* (Pincus, 1990). In the first activity, Trisha identified situations in which she felt guilty, angry, embarrassed, sad, and hurt. Next, she examined what she was thinking about herself or the situation when she had a particular feeling.

In the second activity, Trisha learned that how she thinks affects the way she feels about a situation and was taught how to change her feelings by changing her thoughts. The counselor had Trisha demonstrate her understanding of these concepts by a role play in which the counselor pretended to be an embarrassed teenager and Trisha helped the counselor see that her embarrassment was caused by her thoughts that "everyone in the hallway saw her bump into the trash can; everyone in the whole school must think she is clumsy; no other teenager ever has problems like this." After discussing how feelings are affected when thoughts are negative or blown out of proportion, Trisha learned she could control her vulnerable feelings by thinking more sensibly.

Evaluation

Trisha was a very eager client. After several sessions, the counselor increased the time between appointments and invited Trisha to participate in a small group dealing with teenage self-esteem issues. In the individual sessions, they continued to work on how to apply what she had learned to specific emotional issues.

OTHER TYPICAL EARLY ADOLESCENT CONCERNS

As previously stated, the transition from childhood to adolescence, generally labeled *early adolescence*, is characterized by tremendous change (Petersen, Kennedy, & Sullivan, 1991). During this period, the adolescent knows that most things will be changing, but has no idea how things will turn out, accounting for the prevalent anxiety during this phase of development. Although a good deal of stress is associated with this period that some adolescents find overwhelming and difficult, others see this as a stimulating period that presents challenges and opportunities for growth (Petersen et al., 1991).

Part of the difficulty during this period is that there are simultaneous changes occurring. For example, as they experience puberty, early adolescents also confront other developmental changes, such as changing school structure and format, experiencing more pressure from peers to try new things, and dealing with parents' responses to their pubertal changes, which often have implications for the parents' aging and their own thoughts of impending separation from their child (Petersen, 1987). Additional problems typically experienced are described subsequently in order of intensity with accompanying behaviors that may help identify the problem (Youngs, 1985).

Seventh Grade

Fear of being selected last, interpreted as being unpopular; fear of being chosen first and having to lead (introvert or extrovert behavior is evident; shows extreme shyness or boldness); fear of the unknown related to sexuality (observation of peers, personal exploration and information seeking concerning sexuality, shares myths and rumors about sexuality); extreme concern about being happy or unhappy (inconsistent behavior, loner, introvert, extrovert, periods of depression); fear of not being able to complete schoolwork (procrastination, perfectionism); fear of the school calling home (defensiveness, overly concerned).

Eighth Grade

Fear of being selected first and having to lead, and fear of being selected last and feeling unpopular (extremely shy or bold behavior; introvert or extrovert behavior); fear of dealing with own sexuality (examines self as sexual being; explores facts and information about sexuality); extreme worry about emotional happiness and unhappiness (avoids dealing with specific issues and rejects feelings associated with being unhappy); fear of activities that involve exposing the body (absent from activities; shy or crude about sexuality); fear of being in ninth grade or of not passing (may appear tough or withdrawn; shows interest in grades, but may not use information).

Ninth Grade

Fear of dealing with own sexuality (continues sexual exploration); fear of activities requiring bodily exposure (shy or crude about sex; pretends to be sick on physical education days); extreme worry about being happy or unhappy (avoids dealing with specific issues, rejects negative feelings); fear of being sent to the office, being confronted by a teacher, or getting bad grades (compromises, cooperates, feels embarrassed or defensive; teacher pleaser or overly defensive; renewed commitment to schoolwork); fear of being confronted by someone of the same sex (uses poor reasoning skills; lacks good communication skills).

SUMMARY

In our culture, although no rite of passage marks the transition from childhood to adulthood, early adolescence initiates this process. The changes in physical, intellectual, social, emotional, self, and moral processes are dramatic. Although developing an identity is a critical task at this stage, as well as in adolescence proper, there is a fine line between how much dissent is necessary to achieve a separate sense of self and how much of it is unhealthy risk taking resulting in self-destructive behaviors that may have long-term negative consequences (Baumrind, 1987).

Healthy adolescent development is fostered by providing a prolonged supportive environment during early adolescence, with gradual steps toward autonomy (Irwin, 1987). Successful completion of developmental tasks at this level positively influences the 15- to 18-year-old.

REFERENCES

Adelson, J., & Doehrman, M. J. (1980). The psychodynamic approach to adolescence. In J. Adelson (Ed.), *Handbook of adolescent psychology* (pp. 99–116). New York: Wiley.

Akeroyd-Guillory, D. (1988). A developmental view of anorexia nervosa. *The School Counselor, 36,* 24–33.

Anolik, S. A. (1981). Imaginary audience behavior and perceptions of parents among delinquent and nondelinquent adolescents. *Journal of Youth and Adolescence, 10,* 443–454.

Barrish, I. J., & Barrish, H. H. (1989). *Surviving and enjoying your adolescent.* Kansas City, MO: Westport.

Baumrind, D. (1987). A developmental perspective on adolescent risk taking in contemporary America. In C. E. Irwin (Ed.), *Adolescent social behavior and health* (pp. 93–125). San Francisco, CA: Jossey-Bass.

Berger, K., & Thompson, R. (1991). *The developing person through childhood and adolescence.* New York: Worth.

Berndt, T. J. (1982). The features and effects of friendship in early adolescence. *Child Development, 53,* 1447–1460.

Berndt, T. J. (1989). Obtaining support from friends in childhood and adolescence. In D. Belle (Ed.), *Children's social networks and social supports* (pp. 308–311). New York: Wiley.

Berndt, T. J. (1992). *Child development.* Orlando, FL: Harcourt Brace Jovanovich.

Bireley, M., & Genshaft, J. (1991). *Understanding the gifted adolescent.* New York: Teachers College Press.

Brooks-Gunn, J., & Warren, M. P. (1989). Biological and social contributions to negative affect in young adolescent girls. *Child Development, 60,* 40–55.

Bukatko, D., & Daehler, M. W. (1992). *Child development: A topical approach.* Boston, MA: Houghton Mifflin.

Canfield, J., & Wells, H. (1976). *100 ways to enhance self-concept in the classroom.* Englewood Cliffs, NJ: Prentice-Hall.

Colangelo, N., & Dettmann, D. F. (1985). Characteristics of moral problems and solutions formed by students in grades 3–8. *Elementary School Guidance and Counseling, 19,* 260–271.

Colby, A., Kohlberg, L., Gibbs, J., & Lieberman, M. (1983). A longitudinal study of moral development. *Monographs of the Society for Research in Child Development, 48* (1–2, Serial No. 200).

Colten, M. E., & Gore, S. (1991). *Adolescent stress: Causes and consequences.* New York: Aldine de Gruyter.

Dreikurs, R., & Grey, L. (1970). *A parents' guide to child discipline.* New York: Hawthorn.

Dusek, J. B. (1991). *Adolescent development and behavior.* Englewood Cliffs, NJ: Prentice-Hall.

Eichoness, M. (1989). *Why can't anyone hear me? A guide for surviving adolescence.* Sepulveda, CA: Monroe.

Elkind, D. (1974). *Children and adolescents: Interpretive essays on Jean Piaget.* New York: Oxford University Press.

Elkind, D. (1984). *All grown up and no place to go: Teenagers in crisis.* Reading, MA: Addison-Wesley.

Elkind, D. (1988). *The hurried child: Growing up too fast too soon.* Reading, MA: Addison-Wesley.

Elkind, D., & Bowen, R. (1979). Imaginary audience behavior in children and adolescents. *Developmental Psychology, 15,* 38–44.

Erlanger, E. (1988). *Eating disorders: A question and answer book about anorexia nervosa and bulimia.* Minneapolis, MN: Lerner.

Frank, A. (1963). *The diary of a young girl.* New York: Washington Square Press.

Frisch, R. E. (1991). Puberty and body fat. In R. M. Lerner, A. C. Petersen, & J. Brooks-Gunn (Eds.), *Encyclopedia of adolescence* (pp. 355–392). New York: Garland.

Garfinkel, P. E., & Garner, D. W. (1982). *Anorexia nervosa: A multidimensional perspective.* New York: Brunner/Mazel.

Garfinkel, P. E., & Garner, D. W. (1984). *Handbook of psychotherapy for anorexia and bulimia.* New York: Guilford.

Gibbs, J. C., & Schnell, S. V. (1985). Moral development "versus" socialization: A critique. *American Psychologist, 40,* 1071–1080.

Gold, M., & Petronio, R. J. (1980). Delinquent behavior in adolescence. In J. Adelson (Ed.), *Handbook of adolescent psychology* (pp. 495–535). New York: Wiley.

Irwin, C. E. (1987). *Adolescent social behavior and health.* San Francisco, CA: Jossey-Bass.

Johnson, W., & Kottman, T. (1992). Developmental needs of middle school students: Implications for counselors. *Elementary School Guidance and Counseling, 27,* 3–14.

Klimek, D., & Anderson, M. (1989). *Inner world, outer world: Understanding the struggles of adolescence.* Ann Arbor, MI: ERIC/CAPS.

Knaus, W. (1974). *Rational-emotive education: A manual for elementary school teachers.* New York: Institute for Rational Living.

Larsen, R., & Asmussen, L. (1991). Anger, worry, and hurt in early adolescence: An enlarging world of negative emotions. In M. E. Colten & S. Gore (Eds.), *Adolescent stress: Causes and consequences* (pp. 21–41). New York: Aldine de Gruyter.

Larson, R., & Lampman-Petraitis, C. (1989). Daily emotional states as reported by children and adolescents. *Child Development, 60,* 1250–1260.

LeFrancois, G. R. (1992). *Of children: An introduction to child development.* Belmont, CA: Wadsworth.

Malina, R. M. (1991). Growth spurt, adolescent. In R. M. Lerner, A. C. Petersen, & J. Brooks-Gunn (Eds.), *Encyclopedia of adolescence* (pp. 244–289). New York: Garland.

Newman, B. M., & Newman, P. R. (1991). *Development through life: A psychosocial approach.* Pacific Grove, CA: Brooks/Cole.

Orbach, S. (1986). *Hunger strike: The anorectic's struggle as a metaphor of our age.* New York: W. W. Norton.

Ostrov, E., Offer, D., & Howard, K. L. (1989). Gender differences in adolescent symptomatology: A normative study. *Journal of the American Academy of Child and Adolescent Psychiatry, 28,* 394–398.

Pesce, R., & Harding, C. G. (1986). Imaginary audience behavior and its relationship to operational thought and social experience. *Journal of Early Adolescence, 6,* 83–94.

Petersen, A. (1987). The nature of biological and psychosocial interactions: The sample case of early adolescence. In R. M. Lerner & T. T. Foch (Eds.), *Biological and psychosocial interactions in early adolescence: A life-span perspective* (pp. 35–61). Hillsdale, NJ: Lawrence Erlbaum Associates.

Petersen, A., Kennedy, R., & Sullivan, P. (1991). Coping with adolescence. In M. E. Colten & S. Gore (Eds.), *Adolescent stress: Causes and consequences* (pp. 93–110). New York: Aldine de Gruyter.

Pincus, D. (1990). *Feeling good about yourself: Strategies to guide young people toward more positive, personal feelings.* Carthage, IL: Good Apple.

Powers, S., Hauser, S. T., & Kilner, L. A. (1989). Adolescent mental health. *American Psychologist, 44,* 200–208.

Rest, J. R. (1986). *Moral development: Advances in theory and research.* New York: Praeger.

Rumney, A. (1983). *Dying to please: Anorexia nervosa and its cure.* Jefferson, NC: McFarland.

Santrock, J. (1987). *Adolescence: An introduction.* Dubuque, IA: William C. Brown.

Santrock, J., & Yussen, S. (1992). *Child development: An introduction.* Dubuque, IA: William C. Brown.

Sarafino, E. P., & Armstrong, J. W. (1986). *Child and adolescent development.* St. Paul, MN: West.

Schave, D., & Schave, B. (1989). *Early adolescence and the search for self: A developmental perspective.* New York: Praeger.

Selman, R. (1980). *The growth of interpersonal understanding: Developmental and clinical analyses.* New York: Academic Press.

Silverstein, A., & Silverstein, V. (1991). *So you think you're fat?* New York: HarperCollins.

Simmons, R. G., & Blythe, D. A. (1987). *Moving into adolescence: The impact of pubertal change and school context.* New York: Adline de Gruyter.

Strahan, D. B. (1983). The emergence of formal operations in adolescence. *Transcendence, 11,* 7–14.

Strober, M. (1981). A comparative analysis of personality organization in juvenile anorexia nervosa. *Journal of Youth and Adolescence, 10,* 285–295.

Strub, R. (1990/1991). Concerns I have. In A. Vernon & R. Strub (Eds.), *Developmental guidance program implementation* (pp. 97–98). Cedar Falls, IA: University of Northern Iowa Press.

Tobin-Richards, M. H., Boxer, A. M., & Petersen, A. C. (1983). The psychological significance of pubertal change: Sex differences in perceptions of self during early adolescence. In J. Brooks-Gunn & A. C. Petersen (Eds.), *Girls at puberty: Biological and psychosocial perspectives* (pp. 334–379). New York: Plenum.

Vernon, A. (1988). *P.E.P.S. Psychological education programs for students.* Minneapolis, MN: Burgess.

Vernon, A. (1989). *Thinking, feeling, behaving: An emotional education curriculum for children.* Champaign, IL: Research Press.

Weiner, B., & Graham, S. (1984). An attributional approach to emotional development. In C. E. Izard, J. Kagan, & R. R. Zajonc (Eds.), *Emotions, cognition, and behavior* (pp. 167–191). New York: Cambridge University Press.

Weinhaus, E., & Friedman, K. (1988). *Stop struggling with your teen.* New York: Penguin.

Youngs, B. B. (1985). *Stress in children.* New York: Arbor House.

Youngs, B. B. (1990). *Friendship is forever, isn't it?* Berkeley Springs, WV: Learning Tools.

Youniss, J., & Smollar, J. (1985). *Adolescent relations with mothers, fathers, and friends.* Chicago: University of Chicago Press.

CHAPTER VII

MID-ADOLESCENCE: ASSESSMENT AND INTERVENTION

A parent remarked recently that she thought they had achieved another milestone with their son, aged 15. Instead of insisting that his parents let him out of the car a block from the movie theater so he would not have to be seen with them, they actually had spent an hour together in the shopping center and their son had not even walked several feet behind them. Another parent commented how relieved she was that her teenaged daughter reacted calmly when the mother scorched her daughter's dress for a formal dance. This calmness is what parents hope mid-adolescence brings. Yet, although the "storm and stress" of early adolescence is past, mid-adolescence arrives with new challenges and developmental tasks.

CHARACTERISTICS OF MID-ADOLESCENCE

In mid-adolescence, which corresponds to the high school years ages 15–18 (Baumrind, 1987; Dusek, 1991), the "yo-yo" nature of early adolescence is replaced by greater stability, for the most part (Schave & Schave, 1989). Parents, teachers, and adolescents welcome this change, although, depending on the rate at which they reach formal operational thinking, some adolescents still appear much like early adolescents. Mid-adolescents achieve new freedoms and responsibilities, signified in part by the rite of passage in the form of a driver's license. As my soon-to-be 16-year-old son recently said to me, "Everything's going to change when I get my license!"

Mid-adolescence frequently is described as a period when teenagers try out adult roles (Dusek, 1991), as verified by Havighurst's (1951, reported in Dusek, 1991, p. 7) description of the nine major tasks of adolescence:

>   Stage 1: Accepting one's physical makeup and acquiring a masculine or feminine gender role.

Stage 2: Developing appropriate relations with age mates of both genders.

Stage 3: Becoming emotionally independent of parents and other adults.

Stage 4: Achieving the assurance that one will become economically independent.

Stage 5: Determining and preparing for a career and entering the job market.

Stage 6: Developing the cognitive skills and concepts necessary for social competence.

Stage 7: Understanding and achieving socially responsible behavior.

Stage 8: Preparing for marriage and family.

Stage 9: Acquiring values that are harmonious with an appropriate scientific world picture.

Sroufe and Cooper (1988) summarized these tasks a bit differently, stating that, in addition to achieving an identity that is integrated and unique, adolescents must achieve a new level of trust and closeness with peers, acquire a new status in the family as connections with parents take on a different form, and move toward an autonomous position in relation to the larger world, particularly in terms of career choice.

Dusek (1991) speculated that some of these tasks are more difficult to master in a contemporary society, citing preparing for and entering the job market as an example. As a result, Dusek maintained that adolescents have more trouble becoming adults than their parents did, which may contribute to other problems. Elkind (1988) also posited that it is harder to grow up today, but attributes this to the fact that children are forced to grow up too soon. By the time they reach adolescence, Elkind said, they are ready to experiment with many things that are "off limits" until they reach a certain age, such as drinking and smoking. Elkind noted in particular the rush for sexual experimentation, which results in high teenage pregnancy rates and an increase in sexually transmitted diseases and AIDS (auto immune deficiency syndrome) among teenagers. According to Elkind, other negative ramifications result from this pressure to grow up fast: greater stress, more youth crime and violence, and teenage suicide. Perhaps the most significant implication is that some young people are trying out new behaviors and experiencing things without the necessary level of developmental maturity.

Thus, although some maintain that mid-adolescence is a calmer, more predictable stage of development, social and environmental factors impinge on the developmental process and may affect the "smooth sailing" scenario. Although it is difficult to describe universal patterns of adolescence, because personal circumstances and rates of maturation have a strong impact, the following descriptions provide general trends.

Self-Development

"Who am I?" and "What will I become?" are central to the gradual process of identity development that begins at birth and solidifies during mid-adolescence. The concern with identity becomes important at this time due to several factors. First of all, as a result of puberty, adolescents are more aware of sexual impulses and new sensations. In addition, they are expected to exhibit more responsible behavior and begin channeling this into achievement and competition. There is also an emerging sense of social maturity that encourages speculation about roles in society (Adams & Gullotta, 1983). Through continual self-questioning and a "trying on" of various roles and responsibilities, a sense of identity begins to formulate.

In his classic work *Identity: Youth and Crisis* (1968), Erikson described adolescence as a turning point in life, where young people expend a tremendous amount of energy on issues related to self-definition and self-esteem. According to Erikson, young people attempt to establish themselves as separate individuals and at the same time preserve some connection with meaningful aspects of the past, including family. The process of "finding themselves" involves establishing a moral, sexual, vocational, political, and religious identity. Erikson maintained that identity is achieved through a crisis of emotional stress that requires an alteration in one's viewpoint. The crisis precipitates a change, either forward toward adulthood, or backward toward earlier developmental levels. Although most adolescents are able to deal successfully with the stress and anxiety associated with this crisis, some remain confused and have few commitments to goals or values, whereas others may develop a negative identity, associating with delinquent or antisocial groups (Adams & Gullotta, 1983).

Marcia (1980) identified four major identity statuses: achievement, foreclosure, diffusion, and moratorium. Identity achievement is the desired goal and occurs when adolescents develop their own goals, accepting some values from parents and society, and rejecting others. High self-esteem and self-directedness characterize this status. For some youth, the process of rejecting some values and accepting others is problematic, resulting in premature identity formation called foreclosure. An example of this is the adolescent who decides at any early age to be a teacher, but later in life decides that he really wanted to be a musician. These adolescents generally have low self-esteem, are easily influenced by others, and are very dependent.

Identity diffusion occurs when the adolescent has difficulty meeting the typical demands of adolescence and cannot make friends, complete schoolwork, or make decisions about the future. These youth often have low self-esteem, are dependent, and frequently isolated.

Moratorium generally occurs after mid-adolescence, in college or in the military, for example, when the adolescent takes "time out" to experiment with different identities before deciding on one.

Much of what happens in terms of self-development in mid-adolescence depends on the degree to which formal operational thinking is attained and the level of self-esteem of the early adolescent as he or she enters this next developmental level. Baumrind (1987) and Sroufe and Cooper (1988) contended that after age 13, there is a gradual increase in self-worth, and the self-concept becomes more complex, individuated, and distinct. Adolescents are more self-reflective and think of themselves as a coherent system made up of integrated parts. Baumrind (1987) noted that youth who enter mid-adolescence feeling confident about themselves have a sense of mastery and can deal more effectively with stressful circumstances and emotional issues than can adolescents who have poor self-esteem.

Social Development

The importance of peer relationships continues into mid-adolescence, and the increased time spent with peers serves a variety of functions for the teenager: to try out various roles, to learn to tolerate individual differences as they come in contact with people who have different values and life-styles, and to prepare themselves for adult interactions as they begin to form more intimate relationships (Dusek, 1991).

For the adolescent who has attained formal operational thinking, relationships take on a new dimension. During early adolescence, friendships are focused on activities, and friends are selected on this basis without thought of long-term compatibility. From ages 14 to 16, loyalty and security are important elements in friendship, particularly for females (Berndt, 1982; O'Brien & Bierman, 1988). At this age, friends are an important source of identity and value development, as well as emotional support. Beginning at about age 17, friendships are based more on compatibility and shared experiences, and are chosen on the basis of their contribution to the relationship as well as on personality (Dusek, 1991). O'Brien and Bierman (1988) speculated that there is less need for a confidant and someone to depend on, which increases the adolescents' tendency to appreciate people with differing characteristics.

Intimate friendships with both the same gender and opposite gender increase during mid-adolescence, with females seeking these intimate relationships sooner than males (Buhrmester & Furman, 1987). These kinds of friendships have several positive outcomes for adolescents: they develop more social sensitivity, they become more adept at affective perspective taking, and they are better able to engage in mutually beneficial interactions.

Until age 15 or 16, there is generally more antagonism than attraction toward the opposite gender, although teenagers begin to experience casual heterosexual contact through participation in group activities before actual dating begins (Berger & Thompson, 1991; Berndt, 1992; Dusek, 1991; Sroufe & Cooper, 1988). Although some teenagers start dating earlier, more serious dating generally begins after age 15, with relationships characterized by deep emotional involvement generally developing even later (Dusek, 1991; Sroufe & Cooper, 1988). Likewise, sexual experimentation usually does not begin until mid-adolescence, and, particularly since the 1970s, there has been a trend toward increased sexual activity among high schoolers (Newman & Newman, 1991).

As adolescents first become aware of sexual feelings during mid-adolescence, they also begin to clarify gender orientation (Coleman & Remafedi, 1989). Coleman and Remafedi expressed concern that two central tasks of adolescence, finding an identity and developing intimacy with another individual, easily can be "derailed" by sexual minority status (p. 37). Gay, lesbian, and bisexual adolescents often experience confusion along with hostility and rejection from peers (Gonsiorek, 1988). Parents and adolescents need support in dealing with these issues.

As they become less egocentric, adolescents realize there will be shortcomings in relationships and they are better able to accept this. In turn, they are more likely to stick with a friend through a disagreement and generally approach relationships in a more mature fashion. Although friendships gradually become more stable and less exclusive throughout mid-adolescence, Dusek (1991) noted some gender differences, with female friendships fluctuating more than male friendships. The decline of egocentrism also leads to less need to conform to peers. By mid-adolescence, when they have begun to develop personal values and identity, young people are more willing to express their uniqueness.

Cognitive Development

During mid-adolescence, formal operational thinking continues to develop, although many adolescents and even adults still have not reached this level of thinking (Safarino & Armstrong, 1986; Schave & Schave, 1989; Sroufe & Cooper, 1988). The attainment of formal operational thinking allows the adolescent to think and behave in qualitatively different ways. For example, adolescent thinking is associated with the concept of possibilities. As they become increasingly able to think abstractly, they can distinguish the real and concrete from the abstract and possible. They also can hypothesize, think about the future, be introspective, and combine thoughts (Dusek, 1991; Sroufe & Cooper, 1988). Their thought processes are more flexible; and they are less likely to think in either–or terms, which has a positive effect on how they problem solve.

Development of formal operational thinking has implications for academic success. Adams and Gullotta (1983) noted that students with higher IQ scores are more capable of using complex reasoning strategies. Sroufe and Cooper (1988) reported that formal operational thinking affects performance, particularly in math and science.

Formal operational thinking significantly affects how adolescents think and reason, which in turn relates to other areas of their lives. Although there is variation in the rate at which adolescents develop this ability, studies show that formal operational thinking clearly improves with age (Flexer & Roberge, 1980).

Physical Development

Depending on when the early adolescent begins puberty, physical development in mid-adolescence may continue at a rather rapid rate or gradually begin to slow down. Generally by this time, females have achieved full breast growth and have started to menstruate, pubic hair has developed completely, and their body weight has been redistributed resulting in a more fully developed figure (Newman & Newman, 1991). Although females are more dissatisfied with physical appearance and body image than males, after age 15 they begin to feel more positive (Rauste-von Wright, 1989).

Males generally lag behind females in rate of physical development by approximately 2 years (Berger & Thompson, 1991). Consequently, during early adolescence, females are usually taller than males. During mid-adolescence, this trend is reversed. By age 15, males usually experience a lowering of their voice, and by age 16, facial hair appears. This is viewed as an important "coming of age" event for males: the shaving of the face becomes a significant validation of gender role (Newman & Newman, 1991). Final pubic hair develops at about age 18.

These average ages are simply approximations. Healthy adolescents may be as much as 3 years ahead or behind these ages, and the sequence of changes also may vary somewhat. For example, females may have some pubic hair before their breasts begin to develop, and males may have facial hair before their voices change (Berger & Thompson, 1991).

Genes, nutrition, and the tendency to experience puberty earlier in this contemporary society all affect physical maturation.

Emotional Development

In contrast to the emotional upheaval characteristic of early adolescence, more emotional stability comes in mid-adolescence. Adolescents are better able to deal with emotionally charged issues, because they are less likely to be overwhelmed by their emotions. Because they are not as vulnerable, they are less defensive and more likely to ask for help if needed. This is an important development, because adolescents who are stuck in the concrete operational stage cannot handle overwhelming emotions and, therefore, use denial to deal with the situation. As a result, rather than relying on parents or professionals to help them cope with problems, they try to figure it out themselves, often unsuccessfully, rather than seek assistance and feel ashamed.

The less erratic emotional state depends to a large extent on the degree to which formal operational thinking has developed. This accounts for the wide variation in how adolescents manage emotions. Those who are more emotionally mature have better coping skills and are less likely to be suicidal or resort to drugs and alcohol.

Moral Development

As previously noted, between the ages of 10 and 18 young people grow more in moral reasoning than during any other period of development (Colby, Kohlberg, & Lieberman, 1983). This progress is due to several factors: adolescents' ability to think more abstractly, their questioning of parental values due to their increased psychological maturity, their exposure to a wider array of values through peer group involvement, and personal experiences that force them to make independent decisions.

Teenagers engage in lots of thinking, reasoning, and questioning as they become concerned with broader political, philosophical, and religious matters. Because their thinking is more flexible, they can consider different sides of an issue. As they wrestle with everyday moral issues in their own lives, they are better able to identify consequences. However, this does not always translate into behavior consistent with their ability to reason. For instance, although most adolescents are at the "law and order" stage in Kohlberg's model of moral development, doing what is right and showing respect for authority (Colby et al., 1983; Dusek, 1991; Epanchin & Paul, 1987), it is not uncommon to find adolescents who cheat in school, drink alcohol or use drugs illegally, or exceed the speed limit.

Increasingly during mid-adolescence, teenagers are confronted with moral dilemmas. The peer group, parents, cultural norms, and personal pressures influence the level of moral decision making.

PARENTAL INVOLVEMENT DURING MID-ADOLESCENCE

During this phase of development, adolescents are generally less volatile, resulting in more positive family interaction. Because they are less egocentric, they are more concerned with the feelings of parents and siblings, and have a more "give and take" attitude (Sarafino & Armstrong, 1986; Schave & Schave, 1989).

Although adolescents spend less time with their families, in healthy families adolescents continue to maintain a sense of emotional attachment to them, as verified by Hunter and Youniss (1982). Their study assessed three dimensions of relationships: control, nurturance, and intimacy. Children in Grades 4, 7, 10, and college responded to the questionnaire, and at each age children perceived parents as exerting more control over them than peers. Tenth graders perceived parents to be as nurturant as peers, but perceived relationships with peers to be more intimate than with parents.

Parents continue to be an important source of support and role modeling, and adolescents need parents' experience and guidance for important decisions such as career choices. For many parents, thinking ahead to career choices raises feelings of ambivalence. Although they may realize that their adolescent needs to become independent and leave home, some parents may feel rejected and deal ineffectively with this necessary loss.

PROBLEM ASSESSMENT AND INTERVENTION: SELECTED CASE STUDIES

On a daily basis, helping professionals counsel a wide range of adolescents, from the basically well-adjusted teens who, with minimum intervention, successfully confront the challenges of mid-adolescence to the angry, defiant, or depressed youths whose coping skills are so inadequate that intervention is not always enough. As previously described, the degree to which formal operational thinking is attained influences moral, social, self, and emotional development, and has a major impact on adolescents' perception of the world as they address issues pertinent to this period in their lives.

Problems experienced in mid-adolescence, ages 15–18, are described subsequently, accompanied by assessment strategies and intervention techniques.

Problem One: Fifteen-Year-Old Clarissa

Problem Overview

Clarissa initiated contact with the counselor, because she and her mother had not been getting along. According to Clarissa, her mother was "out of touch" with what kids today were doing, and, because of that, she treated Clarissa like a baby and never let her do anything. Even though she was the oldest child in the family, the only difference in the way she was treated was that she had to do more work around the house. Clarissa's stepfather, who she liked a lot, agreed with everything her mother decided. If Clarissa tried to talk to them about how unfair things were, they reminded her that they knew what was best for her. Clarissa said she thought about this problem all the time and hated to go home. Although this problem had been going on for several months, Clarissa had not rebelled to the point of disobedience and seemed frustrated rather than angry.

Developmental Considerations

Given that this teenager is only 15, it is probable that she has not attained formal operational thinking to the point where her thinking becomes less dichotomous, her emotions stabilize, and her relationships with her parents improve. Parent–child conflict is not at all uncommon at this stage of development, and, in fact, is a vehicle for adolescents to question rules, ideas, and values to form their own identities.

Assessment

To get a picture of the exact nature of the restrictions, the counselor asked Clarissa to make a list of all the things that her friends were allowed to do, but that she was restricted from doing. Next, she asked her to rate each item with an "A" (always) or an "S" (sometimes) to help distinguish if she was always or just sometimes prohibited from these activities. She then asked Clarissa to participate in a role-play activity to determine the dynamics of the interaction when Clarissa was told that she was not allowed to do something. The counselor requested that Clarissa play her mother and she would play Clarissa, selecting an item from Clarissa's list to use as an example.

When the counselor suggested to Clarissa that she would like to interview her mother and stepfather to learn more about the problem, this young woman began to backpedal, stating that they would never come, that they would not be honest, and that there was no point in talking to them, because they would never change. On a hunch, the counselor empathized with Clarissa, stating that there probably was not anything positive about her family, but she asked Clarissa to complete a family "coat of arms" (Canfield & Wells, 1976, pp. 50–51) just to see if there was any hope for change. Clarissa was invited to draw symbols or write words in each of the six spaces in response to the following: (a) something that you and your family enjoy doing together, (b) something you would miss if you did not live with your family, (c) something you and your family laugh about, (d) something you wish would change in your family, (e) a way in which you are like your mother, and (f) a wish for you and your family.

After completing these various assessments, the counselor sensed that Clarissa had positive feelings about her family in general, and was thinking dichotomously when she implied that she never got to do what her friends did. In fact, Clarissa had several "sometimes" responses on her list, but to her it seemed like she had no freedom. The counselor pointed out that, because Clarissa had some positive feelings about her family, they must not be that unreasonable, and perhaps it would help if the counselor could meet with them to solve this problem. Clarissa was skeptical, but agreed.

Intervention

With Clarissa, the counselor first wanted to help her be more realistic about what she requested and what her parents actually forbid her to do. She asked Clarissa to keep a daily chart, on which she wrote the request, the response, and whether she thought the response was reasonable or unreasonable. These data helped Clarissa put the situation in perspective. Next, she adapted an activity called *Should They or Shouldn't They?* (Vernon, 1989), which helped this young client learn to distinguish between reasonable and unreasonable demands and to see the situation from other points of view. For example, Clarissa was given a sorting board and cards with statements such as: parents should let their kids hang out with anyone they want; parents should never ask questions about what their kids are doing; parents should try to be fair; parents should always let their kids have their way; parents should listen to their kids; parents should provide food and shelter for their kids. After reading each card, Clarissa was to place it in the reasonable, unreasonable, or depends category on the board. She and the counselor then discussed whether her requests were reasonable or unreasonable based on these examples.

Clarissa's parents were just as frustrated by the increased antagonism as she was. The counselor explained that developmentally it was normal for their daughter to want to spend more time with peers and also characteristic for Clarissa to overgeneralize about what she was not allowed to do. As the parents shared their rules, it appeared they were being somewhat restrictive, which the counselor attributed to the fact that this was their first teenager and they needed some guidance in negotiating this phase of development. She recommended that they read *How to Stop the Battle with Your Teenager: A Practical Guide to Solving Everyday Problems* (Fleming, 1989), which helps parents understand their teenagers and how to communicate with them about a variety of issues. The counselor also met with them and their daughter to facilitate discussion about privileges.

Evaluation

The facts that this problem had not gotten out of hand with rebellious behavior and that the parents were willing to work on the issue made treatment much more successful. In addition, Clarissa's positive feelings for her parents and her ability to see that she tended to exaggerate the frequency with which she was never allowed to do anything also facilitated problem solving. The counselor continued to work with Clarissa and her parents to ease them through this stage of development.

Problem Two: Sixteen-Year-Old Laurie

Problem Overview

Laurie's boyfriend, Todd, had been threatening to break up with her for the last few weeks. Laurie was devastated. They had been going together all year, but lately he had been ignoring her, saying that he wanted to date other girls. Because he lived an hour away, they only could see each other on the weekends. Although he used to call her during the week, he did not do that very often now. When Laurie tried to call him, he was never home. As a result of this situation, Laurie was not sleeping well, had a hard time concentrating on her schoolwork, and felt terrible.

Developmental Considerations

Dating relationship problems are very common at this age and can be a major source of anxiety. Although there generally is increased comfort around the opposite gender during mid-adolescence, the degree of threat resulting from relationship difficulties is often related to an adolescent's self-concept and his or her level of cognitive functioning, which affects the ability to interpret abstract concepts and problem solve.

Assessment

Laurie was upset and rambled a lot, so it was difficult to keep her focused to get a clear picture of the problem. To help pinpoint specific feelings and thoughts about the upsetting events, the counselor used a worksheet with the following three questions:

1. Describe an upsetting circumstance. What happened? How did you react?
2. Describe how you felt.
3. Describe what you were thinking to yourself about what happened.

Although they did this orally, the structure allowed the counselor to develop a more comprehensive picture of the problem. This young client identified several upsetting events: being stood up, being ignored (lack of phone calls), and constant arguing. Laurie felt angry and upset when Todd ignored her or did not call, but she also felt depressed and upset because they argued so much. Her thoughts were: he must be seeing someone else; I'll never get over this; I do not know what I will do if we break up; he has no right to treat me this way; there must be something wrong with me or he would want to go out with me; if he drops me, I will never find another boyfriend.

To get a sense of how upset and depressed this teenager was, the counselor asked Laurie to keep a feeling chart, rating her moods on an hourly basis from 1 (low) to 10 (high). From this, he noticed that when Laurie was not thinking about Todd, she functioned fairly well, but that thoughts of him were quite pervasive. She denied being suicidal.

In analyzing the information, it appeared that Laurie was involved in a codependent relationship: she was trying to change Todd so he would be more attentive to her, and she was allowing him to control her activities because she stayed home waiting for his phone calls and visits. In addition to her anger at him, Laurie showed her low self-esteem in thinking "there must be something wrong with me or he'd like me better."

Intervention

The counselor first addressed the codependent relationship issues by explaining the concept to this young client and inviting her to list her codependent behaviors in this relationship. Then the counselor used strings tied to his arms and legs and had Laurie pull on them to demonstrate to her that the harder she pulled, the more he resisted, so her attempts to control him did not work and only resulted in further argument.

To address her self-esteem issues, the counselor drew a circle, divided it into six parts, and asked Laurie to label each part as an aspect of herself, such as girlfriend, student, friend, basketball player, musician, and babysitter. Next, Laurie drew a line beside each label and marked it good, bad, or fair in relation to how she felt about herself in each aspect. As the counselor predicted, she felt quite good about herself in each area except as a girlfriend. The counselor used this information to show Laurie that her whole life was not awful, but instead just one aspect.

He also taught her about the concept of mind reading, and encouraged her to ask Todd why he was withdrawing more from the relationship, rather than automatically assuming it was because she was lacking. The counselor also had her do a "reality check" by asking her if there were other males interested in her who did not ask her out because she was going steady. As a final activity, the counselor asked Laurie to list 10 good things about herself, and then challenged her to think about whether she really deserved to be treated this way, helping her identify some positive self-statements such as "I am a good person even if Todd ignores me" and "There are lots of good things about me and I do not have to be treated this way."

As a final strategy, the counselor taught Laurie how to assert herself in relationships and followed this by role playing. He also recommended that she read *Teen Relationships* (Johnson, 1992), an insightful book about relationships, myths about romance, abusive relationships, and how to end relationships.

Evaluation

Relationship problems do not disappear overnight, especially when there are underlying self-esteem issues. Addressing these issues directly was helpful, and it also was enlightening to teach this client about codependent relationships and assertion, which helped Laurie deal with present and future problems.

Problem Three: Seventeen-Year-Old Mike

Problem Overview

Mike's school counselor referred him to the local mental health clinic, because several of Mike's friends told their counselor that Mike had been talking about killing himself. Although Mike denied this when the counselor spoke with him about it, the counselor contacted Mike's father, who made an appointment for him.

Developmental Considerations

According to a recent report by the Children's Defense Fund (Glosoff & Koprowicz, 1990), six teenagers commit suicide daily. Several authors (Allberg & Chu, 1990; Capuzzi, 1988; Crepsi, 1990; Epanchin & Paul, 1987) noted that suicide rates for young people have risen dramatically in recent years. Although this is not a desirable trend, teenage suicide or suicidal behavior is not uncommon and frequently is seen as the only way to deal with pervasive hopelessness.

Evaluation

Mike essentially refused to talk, so the counselor first relied on information from the father, asking him questions indicative of the warning signs of suicide (Capuzzi, 1988; Stefanowski-Harding, 1990): Had there been a sudden decline in school attendance and performance? Had there been a recent loss such as a move, death of a close friend or relative, divorce, breakup with a girlfriend? Was he withdrawing more from peers? Had there been previous suicide attempts to his knowledge? Was he verbally threatening suicide or alluding to how much better things would be if he were not alive? Had there been any recent suicides in Mike's school? Were there other stressors in his life of which his father was aware ? Did Mike drink, smoke, or use drugs? How unusual was this recent behavior?

From the father's responses, the counselor learned that Mike's girlfriend recently had moved to another state and had broken up with him. Because he was a single parent with three younger children, he had not had time to pay a lot of attention to how Mike was behaving. Because he had to work a lot of overtime, the kids were alone much of the time. Their mother had moved out of state several years ago and had very little contact with the boys.

The father said Mike wrote a lot of poetry, so when the counselor met with Mike later in the session, she asked if he would share some of his poems so she could understand how he was feeling and try to help him. Mike agreed, but said he did not need help. The counselor told him she understood this and that she worked with lots of teenagers who felt similarly. She asked Mike to listen to a short tape in which a former suicidal client talked about her feelings and how eventually counseling had helped her. Although Mike had not really admitted to being suicidal, the counselor managed to get him to sign a contract stating that he would not hurt himself and that he would participate in at least three counseling sessions. She also suggested hospitalization and/or medication to the father as an alternative if the problem persisted.

During the following session, Mike shared his poetry with the counselor. He obviously was feeling very dejected because his girlfriend moved and had broken up with him, and was convinced he never would have another meaningful relationship. He saw his future as hopeless. It appeared that he had a suicide plan and, in addition to the situation with his girlfriend, he was not doing as well as he thought he should in school and felt like he was not going to amount to anything. After reading the poetry, the counselor shared a suicidal tendencies scale with Mike, attempting to get his perception of his behavior and thinking relative to the 13-item scale, which assessed dimensions such as self-esteem, support system, depression, will to live, frequency of suicidal thoughts, and external behaviors. Scoring of this scale confirmed the seriousness of this situation.

Intervention

Due to Mike's reluctance to discuss the situation, the counselor used writing as the major intervention. She gave him a sheet of paper with the following unfinished sentences and asked him to write as much as he wanted about each:

1. Things in my life seem hopeless, because _____.
2. Death appeals to me, because _____.
3. If I were dead, other people would feel _____.
4. Life would be worth living if _____ were different.
5. My obituary would say _____.

She then attempted to work with Mike to address the major loss of his girlfriend by asking him to talk about why he thought he never could have another relationship as good as this one. The counselor asked if the girl broke up with him because she did not care about him or because it was not very feasible to have further contact? Why was Mike giving this young woman so much power over his life? The counselor challenged him to think about whether this event was worth wasting his entire future over. She encouraged him to think about the possibility that, at some point in his life, he might have another girlfriend; there is no guarantee that he would not. Furthermore, she pointed out to him that if he were dead, the possibility of another girlfriend would not be feasible.

Challenging this client's thoughts seemed to help somewhat, and Mike left the session promising to read *Teenage Suicide* (Gardner, 1990). In the following sessions, the counselor actively worked with Mike to help him see that the loss of a girlfriend is a relatively normal teenage problem with which he could learn to deal. She encouraged him to continue to use his poetry as a means to express his feelings about what the relationship meant to him. She also helped him look at the other stressors in his life such as his failure to live up to his expectation that he could do better in school and his prediction that he never would amount to anything. The counselor used a forced-field analysis to help Mike identify what was working for and against him in attaining better grades, and together they set goals for change.

Evaluation

Over a period of several weeks and intense counseling, Mike appeared less depressed and admitted that he was less inclined to suicide. However, it was an up and down process and medication continued to be a consideration.

Problem Four: Eighteen-Year-Old Shannon

Problem Overview

Shannon initiated contact with the counselor, because she had no idea what she wanted to do after high school graduation. She was becoming increasingly anxious about it, because her friends seemed to have their plans finalized. She knew she could continue to live at home with her mother and sisters, but realized she eventually had to do something, because her family did not have a lot of money and she felt a strong need to help.

Developmental Considerations

A major concern for high school juniors and seniors is deciding on a career. Given the vast number of occupational choices in contemporary society, this is a much more complex process than for previous generations. Coupled with this is the rising cost of postsecondary education and, in some areas, a depressed economy limits the number of jobs available.

Assessment

Shannon had taken a number of career interest inventories that indicated a preference for the arts, with a strong second in the medical field. She had a B average and had scored in the average range on the ACT. In talking with Shannon, she appeared confused about her values, which the counselor felt was an important first step in deciding on a career. Furthermore, based on her description of what she saw as her options, Shannon had very stereotypical ideas of what young women could do.

To assess what she felt was important to her, the counselor asked Shannon to identify someone she admired (friend, adult, movie star, politician) and list 10 things she knew about this person concerning their interests, financial status, professional occupation, hobbies, and so forth. Next, she was to discuss how she was like or unlike this person. As she talked, the counselor made a list to use as a starting point for clarifying who she was and what was important to her. She also asked Shannon to complete 10 "I am a person who" sentences, and to rank order from most to least important a list of values such as autonomy, money, success, fame, comfort, and security. The counselor also used a number of worksheets from Farr and Christophersen's (1991) book, *Knowing Yourself: Learning About Your Skills, Values, and Planning Your Life*.

Intervention

As the counselor and Shannon analyzed the data from the various activities, they developed a clearer picture of what things were important to this young woman. Following this, the counselor had Shannon keep a career awareness journal to become more attuned to the various dimensions of jobs that she came in contact with, saw on television, read about, or learned through interviews with people. This helped her see the importance of considering multiple dimensions in selecting a career. After having her client do some research about all of the possible jobs available in her areas of interest, the counselor structured some imagery exercises to help Shannon "see" herself in certain occupations. Helping her identify and dispute her stereotypical ideas was an important part of this activity. The counselor used sentence starters: "As a woman I could. . . .; As a man I could . . . .; As a woman I have to. . . .; As a man I have to. . . . " to stimulate discussion about this issue. Finally, she and Shannon identified where Shannon could get the training she needed for several different possibilities.

Evaluation

Deciding on a career or postsecondary plans is not an easy process. Although the values clarification, personal awareness, and research about different jobs was helpful, Shannon continued to work to clarify her plans throughout the remaining few months of high school.

Problem Five: Eighteen-Year-Old Scott

Problem Overview

Scott initially made an appointment to meet with his school counselor, because he needed financial aid forms. When he returned them, he and the counselor briefly discussed what he was planning to do after high school. In response to the counselor's question about whether he was looking forward to graduation, he replied that all of his friends seemed excited, but he had very mixed feelings, because, as he stated, "Nothing will ever be the same again." Sensing that he needed to deal with loss issues, the counselor encouraged him to set up another appointment.

Developmental Considerations

High school graduation represents a significant turning point for most adolescents, but one that is met with mixed emotions. There is a sense of excitement and anticipation about the future, but this also can be a source of anxiety. In addition, there is a degree of loss, saying goodbye to friends and leaving the familiar behind. Often the last few months of high school result in increased parent–child conflict, as the adolescent struggles with his or her ambivalence about leaving home.

Assessment

Scott was not very clear about his feelings or thoughts other than the awareness that everything was going to change. To develop a clearer idea of his concerns, the counselor gave him a sheet of paper divided into two columns. One side was labeled "now" and the other side was labeled "9 months from now." Along the side of the page were the following categories: friends, family, work, school, leisure, place of residence, how time is spent, and money. Scott was asked to randomly write words that came to his mind regarding these categories for the present and the future. As he shared his list, the counselor could pinpoint Scott's perception of loss and his anxieties more specifically. He also asked Scott to indicate whether these issues were of high, medium, or low concern to him, so the counselor could determine if this was a normal developmental problem or something more severe. Scott described it as more of a "nagging concern" that was not terribly strong, but enough to bother him.

Intervention

To work on the loss issue, the counselor had Scott list the people he would miss the most. Because Scott liked art, the counselor invited him to draw pictures or use photographs to make a collage of some of his happiest memories with these people. The collage, a concrete way to remember these people, was something Scott could take with him and look at when he went away to technical school. The counselor and Scott also talked about ways to have meaningful closure with these people. Scott decided once again to use art and make cards for some of the teachers, female peers, and other adults who were significant to him. He was hesitant about doing this with his male friends, because they might think it was too sentimental, but the counselor suggested that he could make the cards, but not send them. In this way, he could express how he felt and perhaps, when the time was right, he could follow through and share them. Together they identified some meaningful activities that Scott could initiate with these buddies, such as camping out or having one last backyard basketball game.

To deal with the anxiety about the future, the counselor summarized the data from the assessment exercise and listed the concerns: financial (not enough money, will I find a job); friends (will I make any new friends and how); and school (am I smart enough to make it). He then asked Scott to describe how he had dealt with these concerns in the past and which strategies he could continue to use. The counselor had Scott examine his academic record and previous performance in difficult subjects that might indicate his chances for success in new areas, and discussed possible sources of support such as the counseling and career placement centers at the technical school. He also gave Scott names of two students who were attending this school, and suggested that Scott contact them and perhaps spend a day with them to get a feel for what it was like before he actually started attending. As a final intervention, he suggested that Scott read *Necessary Losses* (Viorst, 1986).

Evaluation

Because the anxiety primarily was about the future, the counselor did what he could to help Scott examine the facts as well as his previous problem-solving abilities to give him more confidence about dealing with these upcoming issues. Although the counselor knew the concrete activities would help deal with the loss, in reality Scott may continue to grieve periodically as a natural way of working through the issues.

OTHER TYPICAL DEVELOPMENTAL PROBLEMS

As an elementary-aged child, I recall sitting on the couch with my friend watching *American Bandstand* on television. We were weak with envy, watching the teenagers dance to rock and roll, whirling about in their bobby socks, felt skirts, and rolled up shirt sleeves. Later that night, we planned to spy on our teenaged babysitter and her boyfriend who we knew would be "necking" on the porch after they thought we were asleep.

As a helping professional, I sometimes have trouble juxtaposing my memory of what I thought being a teenager was all about with the reality I see with some adolescents today. It is safe to say that life is more complex due to a variety of factors: changing family structures, a faster pace of life, changing values with fewer clear-cut notions of what is right or wrong, and a societal crisis characterized by such things as higher unemployment, conflict, and tension (Thompson & Rudolph, 1992). If we superimpose these factors on normal developmental problems that most adolescents experience to some degree, it is not surprising to see increases in teenage runaways (Sroufe & Cooper, 1988), alcohol and drug abuse (Crabbs, 1989; Thompson & Rudolph, 1992), eating disorders (Akeroyd-Guillory, 1988; Berndt, 1992), teen pregnancy (Sroufe & Cooper, 1988), and teen suicide (Epanchin & Paul, 1987; Thompson & Rudolph, 1992). Although to many teens these behaviors are seen as ways to deal with problems, they become problems.

In addition to these problems that some adolescents experience, career development is a major concern for most young people. According to Super (1957), the high school student is actively involved in career exploration, first in the form of career fantasy about what he or she will be and, later, a reality testing as the adolescent considers such factors as ability, interest, and training requirements. Mitchell (1986) noted that many adolescents feel overwhelmed with the task of making realistic career choices, because the job picture changes so rapidly.

Youngs (1985) identified other, more typical, concerns for the high school student. These are listed by grade level in order of importance as ranked by teenagers, along with behavioral indicators of the issue. Note that concerns for ninth graders were listed in the previous chapter, but, in many school districts, ninth graders are in high school.

Tenth Grade

Fear of being chosen first and having to be a leader, or fear of being picked last (does not risk participating); fear that a peer will steal their boyfriend or girlfriend (jealousy, possessiveness); fear of not getting any meaning out of high school (expresses negative self-concept); fear of participating in athletics, clubs, school projects, or organizations and failing (reluctance or refusal to participate); fear of not completing assignments (cheating); questioning family relationships (may be defensive, ignores the family).

Eleventh Grade

Fear of undressing in a group (introspective); fear of being ridiculed if speaking in front of a group; fear that peers will criticize their physical appearance (seeks reassurance that they are okay); fear of being inadequately prepared for the future (confused about career options); money concerns (may steal; seeks employment); fear of sexual expression or how others view them sexually (withdrawal or heavy experimentation); fear that adults will define roles for them (easily defensive).

Twelfth Grade

Fear that adults will define roles for them (defensive); fear of inadequate training in high school (expresses confusion about career choices); fear of lack of preparation after graduation (may appear irresponsible in actions or decisions); fear of not having enough money (works one or more jobs); fears that he or she is deficient as a learner (disinterested unless activity is perceived as highly relevant).

SUMMARY

Mid-adolescence is a period of development in which many new capacities emerge and existing ones increase. Not only are cognitive skills more powerful, but new types of relationships develop, along with more differentiation of feeling and greater reflection on these feelings. Mid-adolescence serves an important function as a "stepping stone" to the young adult world, where there are even greater challenges and new opportunities.

It is difficult to say whether mid-adolescence is becoming more stressful for the majority of youngsters. It is clear that self-defeating methods of dealing with problems are seen as options more frequently. Conscious efforts at both intervention and prevention will help adolescents negotiate this significant stage of development.

REFERENCES

Adams, G. R., & Gullotta, T. (1983). *Adolescent life experiences.* Monterey, CA: Brooks/Cole.

Akeroyd-Guillory, D. (1988). A developmental view of anorexia nervosa. *The School Counselor, 36,* 24–33.

Allberg, W. R., & Chu, L. (1990). Understanding adolescent suicide: Correlates in a developmental perspective. *The School Counselor, 37,* 343–350.

Baumrind, D. (1987). A developmental perspective on adolescent risk taking in contemporary America. In C. E. Irwin (Ed.), *Adolescent social behavior and health* (pp. 93–125). San Francisco, CA: Jossey-Bass.

Berger, K., & Thompson, R. (1991). *The developing person through childhood and adolescence.* New York: Worth.

Berndt, T. J. (1982). The features and effects of friendship in early adolescence. *Child Development, 53,* 1447–1460.

Berndt, T. J. (1992). *Child development.* Orlando, FL: Harcourt Brace Jovanovich.

Buhrmester, D., & Furman, W. (1987). The development of companionship and intimacy. *Child Development, 58,* 1101–1113.

Canfield, J., & Wells, H. (1976). *100 ways to enhance self-concept in the classroom.* Englewood Cliffs, NJ: Prentice-Hall.

Capuzzi, D. (1988). Adolescent suicide: Prevention and intervention. In J. Carlson & J. Lewis (Eds.), *Counseling the adolescent: Individual, family, and school interventions* (pp. 41–55). Denver, CO: Love.

Colby, A., Kohlberg, L., Gibbs, J., & Lieberman, M. (1983). A longitudinal study of moral development. *Monographs of the Society for Research in Child Development, 48* (1–2, Serial No. 2000).

Coleman, E., & Remafedi, G. (1989). Gay, lesbian, and bisexual adolescents: A critical challenge to counselors. *Journal of Counseling and Development, 68,* 36–40.

Crabbs, M. (1989). Future perfect: Planning for the next century. *Elementary School Guidance and Counseling, 24,* 160–166.

Crepsi, T. D. (1990). Approaching adolescent suicide: Queries and signposts. *The School Counselor, 37,* 256–260.

Dusek, J. B. (1991). *Adolescent development and behavior.* Englewood Cliffs, NJ: Prentice-Hall.

Elkind, D. (1988). *The hurried child: Growing up too fast too soon.* Reading, MA: Addison-Wesley.

Epanchin, B. C., & Paul, J. L. (1987). *Emotional problems of childhood and adolescence: A multidisciplinary perspective.* Columbus, OH: Merrill.

Erikson, E. (1968). *Identity: Youth, and crisis.* New York: W. W. Norton.

Farr, J., & Christophersen, S. (1991). *Knowing yourself: Learning about your skills, values, and planning your life.* Indianapolis, IN: JIST Works.

Fleming, D. (1989). *How to stop the battle with your teenager: A practical guide to solving everyday problems.* New York: Prentice-Hall.

Flexer, B. K., & Roberge, J. J. (1980). IQ, field dependence–independence, and the development of formal operational thought. *Journal of General Psychology, 103,* 191–201.

Gardner, S. (1990). *Teenage suicide.* Englewood Cliffs, NJ: Messner.

Glosoff, H., & Koprowicz, C. (1990). *Children achieving potential: An introduction to elementary school counseling and state-level policies.* Washington, DC: National Conference of State Legislatures; Alexandria, VA: American Association for Counseling and Development.

Gonsiorek, J. C. (1988). Mental health issues of gay and lesbian adolescents. *Journal of Adolescent Health Care, 9,* 114–122.

Hunter, F., & Youniss, J. (1982). Changes in functions of three relations during adolescence. *Developmental Psychology, 18,* 806–811.

Johnson, J. (1992). *Teen relationships.* Minneapolis, MN: Lerner.

Marcia, J. (1980). Identity in adolescence. In J. Adelson (Ed.), *Handbook of adolescent psychology* (pp. 145–185). New York: Wiley.

Mitchell, J. (1986). *The nature of adolescence.* Calgary, Alberta: Detselig.

Newman, B. M., & Newman, P. R. (1991). *Development through life: A psychosocial approach.* Pacific Grove, CA: Brooks/Cole.

O'Brien, S. F., & Bierman, K. L. (1988). Conceptions and perceived influence of peer groups: Interviews with pre-adolescents and adolescents. *Child Development, 59,* 1360–1365.

Rauste-von Wright, M. (1989). Body image satisfaction in adolescent girls and boys: A longitudinal study. *Journal of Youth and Adolescence, 18,* 71–83.

Sarafino, E. P., & Armstrong, J. W. (1986). *Child and adolescent development.* St. Paul, MN: West.

Schave, D., & Schave, B. (1989). *Early adolescence and the search for self: A developmental perspective.* New York: Praeger.

Sroufe, L. A., & Cooper, R. G. (1988). *Child development: Its nature and course.* New York: Knopf.

Stefanowski-Harding, S. (1990). Child suicide: A review of the literature and implications for school counselors. *The School Counselor, 37,* 328–336.

Super, D. (1957). *The psychology of careers.* New York: Harper.

Thompson, C. L., & Rudolph, L. B. (1992). *Counseling children and adolescents.* Pacific Grove, CA: Brooks/Cole.

Vernon, A. (1989). *Thinking, feeling, behaving: An emotional education curriculum for adolescents.* Champaign, IL: Research Press.

Viorst, J. (1986). *Necessary losses.* New York: Ballantine.

Youngs, B. B. (1985). *Stress in children.* New York: Arbor House.

CONCLUSION

I held a 1-year-old this week. As he grabbed my necklace and stuck it in his mouth, I commented to his grandmother how easily one forgets the typical behaviors of children at particular ages. As I selected a birthday card for our son, who will turn 16 next week, it struck me that there is no way to push the pause button on growth and development. In some cases, what literally occurs at one moment in time never will be repeated: losing the first tooth, tying a shoe for the first time, or being asked out for the first date. There are so many "firsts" during the school-aged years that it is hard to account for them all. On reflection, it is apparent that these are the significant stepping stones for later development.

Although stages traditionally have played an important role in the study of development, in recent years researchers have speculated that this concept may be somewhat stringent (Fischer, 1983; Kenny, 1983). According to Fisher (1983), when children enter a new stage, their behaviors do not automatically shift within a short period of time. In addition, environmental factors influence how a child functions in various circumstances. For example, if adults provide specific support, children may be able to function effectively at a higher developmental level in some situations, but without that support their ability to function might be lower. Kenny (1983) noted that, although development occurs gradually, the rate of development is not always the same. There are times when children appear to be learning at a faster or slower pace. Although skills accumulate continuously, there are spurts in development that characterize it as both continuous and discontinuous.

In reality, developmental stages must be seen as indicators of what generally occurs; the concept must be interpreted liberally. When parents and professionals ask, "What is typical?" our response is that we have guidelines, not prescriptions, of what to expect. Although some may find this frustrating, it would be equally disconcerting to neatly sort children into categories based on whether they specifically match the criteria for a particular developmental stage.

The intent of this book was to provide helping professionals with characteristics of children and adolescents across a variety of dimensions: self, social, cognitive, physical, emotional, and moral development. This information can be used in relation to assessment in two ways: as a barometer of where a child is in his or her development, and as an indicator of how to structure developmentally appropriate assessment instruments. The information is also critical in selecting and designing effective intervention strategies that correspond to the child's developmental level.

The significance of developmental theory in working with children and adolescents cannot be underestimated. Although everyone has an individual timetable, characteristics at various stages of development are useful guidelines that should be used in prevention and intervention to help these youngsters achieve their full potential. A quote from Lewis Carroll's (1971) *Alice in Wonderland* summarizes the challenge children and adolescents face in their growing up process:

> Caterpillar:. . . and who are you? Alice: I . . . I hardly know, Sir, just at present—at least I know who I was when I got up this morning, but I think I must have changed several times since then. (p. 16)

Helping professionals and parents are equally challenged as they work with and support young people in their journey through life. A developmental perspective facilitates this challenge.

REFERENCES

Carroll, L. (1971). *Alice in wonderland.* New York: W. W. Norton.

Fischer, K. W. (Ed.). (1983). *Levels and transitions in children's development.* San Francisco, CA: Jossey-Bass.

Kenny, S. L. (1983). Developmental discontinuities in childhood and adolescence. In K. W. Fischer (Ed.), *Levels and transitions in children's development* (pp. 81–95). San Francisco, CA: Jossey-Bass.